Present Yourself

*Using SlideShare to Grow
Your Business*

Kit Seeborg
Andrea Meyer

BEIJING · CAMBRIDGE · FARNHAM · KÖLN · SEBASTOPOL · TOKYO

PRESENT YOURSELF

by Kit Seeborg and Andrea Meyer

Copyright © 2013 Kit Seeborg. All rights reserved.
Printed in the United States of America.

Published by O'Reilly Media, Inc., 1005 Gravenstein Highway North, Sebastopol, CA 95472.

O'Reilly books may be purchased for educational, business, or sales promotional use. Online editions are also available for most titles (safari.oreilly.com). For more information, contact our corporate/institutional sales department: (800) 998-9938 or corporate@oreilly.com.

Editor: Brian Sawyer	**Compositor:** Holly Bauer
Production Editor: Kristen Borg	**Cover Designer:** Edie Freedman
Copyeditor: Rachel Monaghan	**Interior Designer:** Monica Kamsvaag
Proofreader: Kiel Van Horn	**Illustrator:** Rebecca Demarest
Indexer: Bob Pfahler, Potomac Indexing, LLC	

June 2013: First Edition.

Revision History for the First Edition:

2013-05-24   First release

See *http://shop.oreilly.com/product/0636920027584.do* for release details.

Nutshell Handbook, the Nutshell Handbook logo, and the O'Reilly logo are registered trademarks of O'Reilly Media, Inc. *Present Yourself* and related trade dress are trademarks of O'Reilly Media, Inc.

Many of the designations used by manufacturers and sellers to distinguish their products are claimed as trademarks. Where those designations appear in this book, and O'Reilly Media, Inc. was aware of a trademark claim, the designations have been printed in caps or initial caps.

While every precaution has been taken in the preparation of this book, the publisher and authors assume no responsibility for errors or omissions, or for damages resulting from the use of the information contained herein.

ISBN 13: 978-1-449-34236-4

[V]

*For Calvin and Nathan. Every day you make me
the world's proudest mom.*
—Kit Seeborg

*For my husband, Dana, for his patience,
wit, and steadfast support.*
—Andrea Meyer

Contents

Foreword

WHEN KIT TOLD ME she was thinking of writing a book, I was thrilled for her. When I learned that the book was about SlideShare, I was thrilled for SlideShare as well.

As the content editor for SlideShare, Kit has come to understand SlideShare deeply. She understands what motivates the user, what makes their content popular, what brings them back again and again. She has learned this by reviewing thousands of presentations, talking to hundreds of users, whether by email or via Twitter, by conducting interviews or simply running into them at conferences.

When Kit wrote for us, I was struck again and again by her deep understanding of the social web experience and empathy for the people who inhabit such sites—whether to share their content and expertise, or to connect with others. Many people specialize in either consumer or B2B. Kit's understanding bridges individuals and businesses.

If you are considering this book, you are either using social sites to share your content or are planning to start sharing content. Perhaps you have years of content on your hard drive and have been considering how to best put it to use. Or maybe you are doing a startup and want to do marketing without any budget. Or perhaps you want to improve your mid-size company's web footprint. Regardless of the specific goal, there is an art to sharing content and getting noticed on SlideShare. There is no better guide than Kit on your road to discovering how to use SlideShare for fun and profit.

Rashmi Sinha
Cofounder and CEO of SlideShare
San Francisco, California
April 26, 2013

Preface

PRESENTING AN IDEA IS one of oldest ways that people communicate with each other. It is the basis for innovation, collaboration, and, in some cases, survival. Presentations have traditionally focused on presenting an idea, a product, summaries of work, a story, or a myth. Great presenters know that it's not just the content of the message that matters; it's the way in which it is conveyed.

With the introduction of SlideShare in 2006, suddenly presenters could publicly publish and share their PowerPoint presentations. Content creators could now get their presentations in front of many more people than the audience in the room of a live event. In addition, viewers could see how other public speakers designed and constructed the slidedecks. People could publish and consume content all in the same place. This has led to all kinds of shared learning and creativity for public speaking and information design professionals.

Started as "YouTube for PowerPoint," SlideShare is now a full-scale multimedia publishing platform. Its open API allows for partnerships with companies such as SalesForce, HootSuite, and HaikuDeck. With the acquisition of SlideShare by LinkedIn in 2012, a whole new world of opportunities continues to open up. The relationship between presenting oneself or one's company is being integrated into the largest professional social network in the world.

With the growth of a sharing economy and the democratization of content, traffic to SlideShare has steadily increased since its launch. People began to realize that if they had content published on SlideShare and someone searched for their name, the SlideShare account would display in search results ahead of their own website! That's when SlideShare users started to upload presentations, write a blog post on their own sites, and embed the presentation from their SlideShare accounts.

A whole new wave of presentation designers has emerged, from agencies (such as Jess3, Column Five, Slides That Rock, Empowered Presentations, and Ethos3) to individuals (such as Gwyneth Jones, Jonathon Colman, and Paul Saunders) who design their own presentations in addition to working full time. And presentation designers such as David Crandall, Mars Dorian, and Jesse Desjardins have made their mark on the evolution of presentation design style.

Before SlideShare, speakers would offer to send their slidedecks to audience members. That entailed a lot of manual labor and didn't allow for commenting or sharing on social networks. The content creator had no idea whether the slidedeck was viewed or shared with others. Now, when you attend a professional conference or tune in to an online webinar, you will likely hear the presenter say, "The slides will be on SlideShare." As SlideShare continues to add more functionality and sharing capabilities, the power of publishing on its platform increases—all the more reason to create and publish presentations.

As we talked with leaders in presentation design and communications, we heard many stories of creative ways people are using SlideShare. But few people were using the platform to its full potential. Some companies were using it as a key part of their online marketing, but hadn't really thought much about SEO. Others were putting beautiful and cool artistry into their presentation design, but weren't using tags and keywords to generate traffic to their channels. How can we get people and businesses to use all of the capabilities that SlideShare offers, and build their businesses—be they corporations, individuals, students, nonprofits, or startups? We agreed that we needed to create something that was not only informative, but also useful.

So here it is: not just a handbook for using SlideShare, but a comprehensive guide for incorporating presentations into all aspects of your communications.

Now get out there and present yourself!

Who This Book Is For
This book is intended for:
- Companies of all sizes—from large corporations to small businesses and startups—that want to use the full capabilities of SlideShare to connect with their customers and grow their businesses.
- Professionals in all industries who want to showcase their expertise and build their personal brand to get promotions, new jobs, and new opportunities.

- Governments (local, state, and national) as well as nonprofits that want to inform and report to their constituencies, boards, and existing and potential donors.
- Marketers, professional speakers, and business owners in particular will learn how to include presentations in all aspects of a business and how to use SlideShare as an essential tool in marketing and growing their organizations.

How to Use This Book

If you're new to SlideShare, Chapter 2 will guide you through the registration process and get you quickly to uploading presentations. But even if you are already using SlideShare, that chapter is still worth a look, because it includes some great ways to use SlideShare that you might not have thought of.

This isn't a design book. We defer to the brilliance of Nancy Duarte, Garr Reynolds, Bruce Gabrielle, and Carmine Gallo for presentation design guidance.

Present Yourself is designed to be a useful reference and inspiration as you discover new opportunities to use presentations. Each chapter contains "Real-World Example" sidebars, case studies of how companies and individuals are using SlideShare. You can read the book all the way through, but we also hope that you'll keep it on hand for ideas and information as your career or organization evolves. We will continue to post updates about SlideShare and presentations in general on the book's website:

http://www.presentyourselfbook.com

The book is organized into the following chapters:

Chapter 1: Visual Thinking in Business

This chapter explains the trends toward visual communication in business. It explores the technologies that make visual communication possible and how these trends impact presentation design.

Chapter 2: Getting Started

This chapter walks you through the steps of opening a SlideShare account, uploading presentations, and sharing them with others. It describes the power of sharing, as well as the features and benefits of upgrading to a PRO account.

Chapter 3: Events and Public Speaking

Events and public speaking play a key role in building community and thought leadership for your organization and for your career. This chapter shows how SlideShare is used in all stages of event planning and execution.

Chapter 4: Content Marketing

This chapter focuses on the elements of content marketing that make it effective. You'll learn how presentations, storytelling, and curation fit into a content marketing strategy. The chapter includes case studies of how successful companies are using SlideShare in their content marketing strategies to build their brands and increase SEO.

Chapter 5: Sell, Sell, Sell

There is more to a sales presentation than just a pretty PowerPoint. This chapter explains how to incorporate research, prospecting, and closing the sale into presentation strategy.

Chapter 6: Research and Collaboration

In this chapter, you'll learn how to use SlideShare for research and how sharing presentations on SlideShare is an effective method of collaborating within teams and between companies and their clients.

Chapter 7: Recruiting, Hiring, and Getting Hired

This chapter examines trends in job search, personal branding, résumés, and career management. It delineates how to use presentations in recruiting and how presentations can differentiate you or your company in the job market.

Chapter 8: Organizational Outreach and Communication

This chapter showcases the ways that startups, nonprofits, journalists, and government agencies use SlideShare to meet their business needs. You'll learn the role of presentations in each of these areas and see case studies of each in action.

Why We Wrote This Book (from Kit)

I started reading Rashmi Sinha's blog in 1999, when she was a researcher at UC Berkeley after receiving her PhD in cognitive neuropsychology from Brown University. In 2006, we met in person at the Information Architecture Summit in Vancouver, B.C. This was the same year that she, her brother Amit Ranjan, and her husband Jon Boutelle started working on an idea they called SlideShare. From a shared office in Mountain View, Rashmi and Jon collaborated with Amit, who was building the development team in New Delhi, India. The idea grew into a company and the office moved north to San Francisco.

I would periodically travel to San Francisco for meetings and crash at Rashmi and Jon's apartment in the Mission District. One Sunday morning in 2010, Rashmi and I were talking about how to build SlideShare's presence on social networking platforms and Rashmi asked, "Why don't you do this for us? We haven't had the bandwidth to give Facebook, Twitter, and the blog enough attention. You could do it." So I did.

By posting updates, news, and links to interesting articles about presentation design and delivery, I developed a deeper sense of what the SlideShare community responded to. Across the board, public speakers and presenters, no matter what discipline they come from, simply want to be better. The content-creating community of SlideShare is a living, breathing entity that is constantly growing, improving, and learning from its members. They want to do everything they can to get their ideas conveyed accurately, so that they may be understood. They want to reach the widest audience possible and have their ideas influence people and businesses. And, conversely, the audience wants the presenter to do well. People want to learn and understand new ideas and concepts. They want to be inspired so that they themselves can do better.

This need and desire from the community to learn how to use SlideShare more completely, as well as create and deliver presentations, inspired the idea to create a book. Early in 2012, I interviewed Nancy Duarte about her firm's new tool, Diagrammer. We began talking about the changing trends in presentation design and delivery. That conversation, along with Rashmi, Jon, and Amit's full support, put wind in my sails for writing this book.

There are many talented writers in the US. But there was only one person who I knew had the skill and experience to collaborate with me on this project: Andrea Meyer. Andrea is a prolific writer for the likes of MIT, Harvard Business School, Cisco, and IBM. We met every week for months, on Pearl Street in Boulder, often at Kimbal Musk's The Kitchen Next Door. We originally set out to create a handbook, a guide to using SlideShare. We quickly found that there is far more to using SlideShare, and presentations overall, than would be satisfied by a how-to guide.

Safari® Books Online

Safari Books Online (*http://my.safaribooksonline.com*) is an on-demand digital library that delivers expert *content* in both book and video form from the world's leading authors in technology and business. Technology professionals, software developers, web designers, and business and creative professionals use Safari Books Online as their primary resource for research, problem solving, learning, and certification training.

Safari Books Online offers a range of *product mixes* and pricing programs for *organizations, government agencies,* and *individuals.* Subscribers have access to thousands of books, training videos, and prepublication manuscripts in one fully searchable database from publishers like O'Reilly Media, Prentice Hall Professional, Addison-Wesley Professional, Microsoft Press, Sams, Que, Peachpit Press, Focal Press, Cisco Press, John Wiley & Sons, Syngress, Morgan Kaufmann, IBM Redbooks, Packt, Adobe Press, FT Press, Apress, Manning, New Riders, McGraw-Hill, Jones & Bartlett, Course Technology, and dozens *more.* For more information about Safari Books Online, please visit us *online.*

How to Contact Us

Please address comments and questions concerning this book to the publisher:

O'Reilly Media, Inc.
1005 Gravenstein Highway North
Sebastopol, CA 95472
800-998-9938 (in the United States or Canada)
707-829-0515 (international or local)
707-829-0104 (fax)

We have a web page for this book, where we list errata, examples, and any additional information. You can access this page at:

http://oreil.ly/present-yourself

To comment or ask technical questions about this book, send email to:

bookquestions@oreilly.com

For more information about our books, courses, conferences, and news, see our website at *http://www.oreilly.com*.

Find us on Facebook: *http://facebook.com/oreilly*
Follow us on Twitter: *http://twitter.com/oreillymedia*
Watch us on YouTube: *http://www.youtube.com/oreillymedia*

Acknowledgments

We'd like to thank the following people who made themselves available for interviews: Alex Osterwalder, Felice Frankel, Dean Meyers, Thierry de Baillon, Adam Tratt, Liz Ngonzi, Justin Fogarty, Anna Richter, Catherine Dold, Nikos Sarilakis, Jeremiah Owyang, Samantha Starmer, Scott Schwertly, Rand Fishkin, Beth Hayden, Koka Sexton, Jake Wengroff, Kevin Fisher, Marcy Phelps, Marcia J. Rodney, Ellen Naylor, Rachel Bates Wilfahrt, Joe Chernov, Janet Corral, Sebastian Majewski, Bill Scott, Jason Alba, Jesse Desjardins, Amber Case, Andrew Hyde, Bruce Gabrielle, Ef Rodriguez, and Tara Hunt.

We'd also like to thank Mark Frauenfelder, Baratunde Thurston, Nancy Duarte, Peter Morville, and Dan Pacheco, who generously shared their networks and made introductions for us early on. Thanks to Laurie Lamar for her brilliant insights on information design, and to Klaus Holzapfel, who built the book's digital presence.

And for their help, generosity, and spirit of community, we'd like to thank Laurie Lamar, Beth Kanter, David Crandall, Jonathon Colman, Jose Briones, Amy Sample Ward, Christian de Neef, Todd Zaki Warfel, Abby Covert, Dave McClure, Mandy Jenkins, Rohit Bhargava, Steve Buttry, and Jim Long.

We'd also like to give a special thanks to our editor, Brian Sawyer, for his diligent editorial help as well as his production advice.

Finally, we'd like to thank the SlideShare teams in San Francisco and New Delhi, and especially Kevin Fisher, Ben Woodward, and Amit Sawhney, who reviewed specific chapters and gave us valuable feedback. And, of course, thanks to Rashmi, Amit, and Jon, who started it all.

Visual Thinking in Business

VISUAL THINKING HAS BECOME more important in business, because we're processing much more information than ever before. In addition, much of that information is nonlinear. As a result, slide presentations have become the language of business.

As Alex Osterwalder, author of the international bestseller *Business Model Generation* (Wiley), says, "Visual thinking tools help clarify concepts, be they strategy, operations, or new business models." These visual thinking tools are pictures, sketches, diagrams—anything that quickly conveys an idea or process.

The value of the visual medium is twofold, stemming from:

- The volume of meaningful information that can be succinctly conveyed
- The approachability of images

"It's with visual language—such as pictures and graphics—that we can help people feel less intimidated," says MIT scientist Felice Frankel, a science photographer. That accessibility of images encourages the participation and collaboration vital to solving the problems of today, whether those problems are business problems or societal ones.

Visual Information Is Easier to Process

Humans are naturally visual creatures. "Fundamentally, our visual system is extremely well built for visual analysis," says Noah Iliinsky, coauthor of *Designing Data Visualizations* and *Beautiful Visualization* (both O'Reilly). We're tuned to spot patterns. Consider *Anscombe's quartet*, created by statistician Francis Anscombe, shown in Figure 1-1. First, look at the datasets.

FIGURE 1-1

The x values are the same for the first three datasets.

Anscombe's Quartet							
I		II		III		IV	
x	y	x	y	x	y	x	y
10.0	8.04	10.0	9.14	10.0	7.46	8.0	6.58
8.0	6.95	8.0	8.14	8.0	6.77	8.0	5.76
13.0	7.58	13.0	8.74	13.0	12.74	8.0	7.71
9.0	8.81	9.0	8.77	9.0	7.11	8.0	8.84
11.0	8.33	11.0	9.26	11.0	7.81	8.0	8.47
14.0	9.96	14.0	8.10	14.0	8.84	8.0	7.04
6.0	7.24	6.0	6.13	6.0	6.08	8.0	5.25
4.0	4.26	4.0	3.10	4.0	5.39	19.0	12.50
12.0	10.84	12.0	9.13	12.0	8.15	8.0	5.56
7.0	4.82	7.0	6.42	7.0	6.42	8.0	7.91
5.0	5.68	5.0	4.74	5.0	5.73	8.0	6.89

There seems to be little difference between the datasets. But, when they're graphed out, as shown in Figure 1-2, we suddenly see dramatic differences.

FIGURE 1-2

This is how Anscombe's datasets appear when graphed.

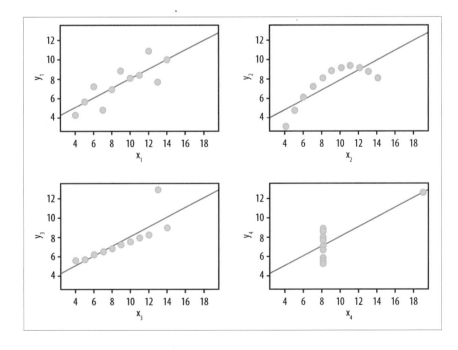

Not only do humans like images, but we're also more efficient thinkers when we use them. As *Mindjet's* Nicola Frazer-Reid reports *(http://min.dj/RJIcmF)*, a study conducted by Mindlab International at the Sussex Innovation Centre investigated how office workers manage existing data using traditional software and how efficient that process is. One of the key findings of the research suggests that when carrying out routine, everyday tasks in the office, if the data is displayed more visually (such as through visual maps), individuals are 17% more productive and need to use 20% fewer mental resources. What's more, teams collaborating on a joint project use 10% fewer mental resources and are 8% more productive when using visualization tools.

Why is visual information easier to process? Dr. Lynda Shaw, a registered chartered psychologist with the British Psychological Society and a Fellow of the Royal Society of Medicine, explains the science behind why we grasp images faster:

> [The brain] stores information in sensory cortical areas and reconstructs meaning based on previously obtained knowledge, tied together by a complex web of connections. Visual mapping emulates this process with visual items that engage more areas of the brain, allowing us to see, explore and understand large amounts of data at once and convey abstract information in intuitive ways.

In short, our brains are finely tuned to process dense visual information faster than other kinds of information. We can grasp more meaning more quickly from an image than from words. The old adage "a picture is worth a thousand words" proves to have a basis in biological fact.

Evolution of Visual Thinking

Verbal abilities developed much later on the evolutionary scale than visual ones. "We are well-developed in imagery for quick environmental awareness," writes Steven Kim in *The Essence of Creativity* (Oxford University Press). According to Kim, imagery has two main advantages. First, we can see multiple things in parallel. For example, we can see the body language of four people simultaneously much better than we can track four conversations at a party simultaneously. Second, we can grasp an image's meaning faster, which accelerates productivity.

Given the growth of big data, the ability to take large amounts of information and present it in a simple, easy-to-read manner is a skill in great demand. Indeed, Dr. Frankel sees a whole new discipline emerging, a "multi-disciplined visual profession."

Visualizations amplify our cognition. Interacting with visualizations helps us think about the information better, because it lightens the cognitive load of memory. We don't have to remember a whole series of numbers, such as in Figure 1-1, but instead can just remember a pattern, as shown in Figure 1-2.

Taking advantage of peoples' visual processing prowess, enterprise software has executive dashboards that use dials or speedometers of red/yellow/green indicators to show you status at a glance. Barcodes and pie charts show relationships. Graphs show trends. That's how we can get by in today's information-overload world. "If we look at a sea of numbers, we quickly get lost, but seeing those numbers displayed as graphs lets us explore and understand the data and its implications," says Stephen Few, author of *Now You See It* and *Show Me the Numbers* (both Analytics Press).

For speakers who use slide presentations and businesses that want to convey ideas to potential customers, this is good news. Technology has evolved to let us convey and transmit visual images much more broadly than we could in the past. "Images engage us in ways that words cannot," Frankel writes with coauthor Angel DePace in their new book, *Visual Strategies* (Yale University Press).

The importance of images to business can't be overstated. As Adam Bly, founder and editor-in-chief of *Seed* magazine, says, "We are a visual society, and the images are as important as the ideas."

Accessibility of Images

Images can jumpstart communication by creating a common language, which can be useful for introducing new customers to your company's products or services, particularly if they're advanced, technological, or new.

In addition, the visual language of pictures and graphics breaks down the barriers of jargon, discipline-related terminology, and language, making it possible for nonexperts or nonnative speakers to understand, provide input, and collaborate. Images are inclusive because they are understandable and approachable.

As a tool for business, the approachability of images means that people can point to a picture and ask about it. As Chapter 6 explores in more detail, this makes visualizations and slides powerful tools for collaboration.

In addition, drawing something helps you figure it out. David Macaulay, bestselling author and illustrator of *The Way Things Work* (Houghton Mifflin) and 24 other highly illustrated books, says, "When you draw something, you really have to look at it. And when you really look at it, you can't avoid thinking about it." Macaulay uses drawing to question, clarify, and think about things.

Macaulay's books are primarily images, interspersed with words. "How great is it to have those two languages to work with and pick and choose from?" Macaulay says. Slide presentations give your business the same advantage.

Visual Objects

In business, how a company makes money (its business model) can be a complex concept to convey to investors, employees, and other stakeholders. Business models have many interrelated moving pieces, which makes them hard to talk about. People can easily miss a key relationship or interdependency when creating or modifying a business model. And with so much complexity and so many possibilities for different kinds of business models, it's easy for coworkers to misunderstand each other as they try to invent new business models.

To understand more closely how to use visual objects and tools, let's use Alex Osterwalder's Business Model Canvas as an example. Shown in Figure 1-3, the Business Model Canvas is a visual tool that helps structure a team's thinking about business models.

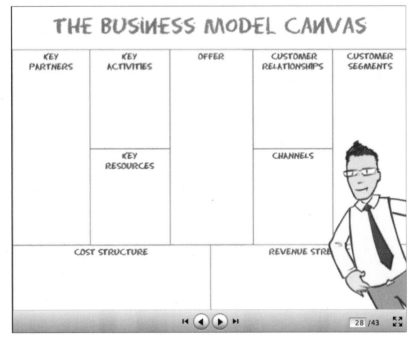

FIGURE 1-3
Osterwalder's Business Model Canvas helps structure a team's thinking about business models.

The first principle of using visual tools and objects is to encourage people to sketch, not just to make lists of words. "Any problem can be made clearer with a picture," Osterwalder says. The sketch, as a "visual artifact," lets people react to something concrete. To encourage people who think they can't draw, Osterwalder points out that people can interpret a stick figure more easily than an abstract concept. "Drawing something, however badly, makes an abstract concept concrete, giving people an opportunity to react to it," he says. In this way, visual tools and visual thinking help business people with understanding, dialogue, exploration, and communication.

Using visual ideas and tools also makes it easy to move concepts around. For example, Osterwalder encourages using large stickies, such as Post-it® notes or Stattys, because people can move them around as they decide where to put the business ideas on the canvas, as shown in Figure 1-4.

FIGURE 1-4

Sticky notes provide flexibility when we're capturing business ideas.

Participants can write ideas—such as who the customer is, the value proposition, and so forth—on stickies, which team members can affix to the canvas and easily move around as they figure out where on the canvas they belong. "Post-it notes are like containers of ideas," Osterwalder says, that can be easily picked up and moved around. They make it easy for people to reconfigure their business models as they refine their thinking and test out new options. The Business Model Canvas helps a team think through its business model. More generally, businesses can use whiteboards or walls and tack posters or stickies onto them as placeholders for ideas.

Finally, the value of using a visual tool is that you can determine in advance the "buckets" that need to be filled in. This helps you avoid missing a key ingredient. In the case of the Business Model Canvas, the canvas lays out the key aspects of a business model, and by seeing it visually, people can quickly spot a missing component.

Because business models are so complex, with many interlocking pieces, it's hard to hold all the pieces in memory and see their interactions and dependencies. The canvas helps everyone see all the pieces and confirm that they work together and make sense. Team members can use different colors of Post-it® notes for different business models, which lets them compare alternate models on the same canvas. This side-by-side comparison can help them pick the most promising model to test.

In summary, the canvas has a visual grammar that tells you where to put something. It lets you capture the big picture while simplifying it, and it lets you see the interdependencies between functions, processes, or ideas. It makes assumptions explicit and creates a visual language that triggers ideas and helps you think through a complex business model systematically. Similarly, visual tools in general make it easier to discuss and convey new business ideas to a company's employees, customers, or investors. In the case of nonprofits and government agencies, visual objects and tools let the public understand and participate in the agencies' actions.

Visual Note Taking

The rise of *note taking* exhibits further evidence of the trend toward more visual thinking in business. Visual note taking is the art of drawing a visual record of a meeting or conference while it is taking place. Some graphic note takers use large-format pages (8 feet × 20 feet) to document an event. Others, like Peter Durand, use an iPad hooked up to a projector screen, drawing notes in real time that are projected alongside or behind the speaker as he or she talks.

See the "Real-World Example" sidebar on Dean Meyers for a look at visual note taking and graphic facilitation in action.

Dean Meyers

Visual problem solver and strategist Dean Meyers is both a graphic recorder and a graphic facilitator, and he takes visual notes both in large format and on the iPad. For example, Dean has taken visual notes at the World Business Forum in large formats, and he used iBrushes on the iPad to take visual notes at the Business Innovation Factory Summit. The iBrushes tool records the order of the brushstrokes and then can re-create them in order, so that participants can later watch a video of the drawing come to life.

"In the real-time event, it adds tremendous value to attendees by increasing participants' memory skill," Dean says. "It's funny that when the boards come to life, it tends to amplify the presentation as it's going on. It gives the attendees stronger memories."

Visual note taking is not merely illustrative, however, and the art is less dependent on ability to draw than it is on ability to synthesize. "Synthesis is critically important," Dean says.

The most successful graphic note takers are the ones who have the strongest ability to synthesize information, to sum everything up. The note taker's ability to summarize and synthesize gives the visual notes a contextual meaning. Visual note takers find an overarching theme or relationships in the anecdotes that are being told and encapsulate them in an impactful way.

FIGURE 1-5
Dean Meyers's graphic recordings of Michael Duarte's workshop at the PopTech Conference are cleaned up and organized for sharing.

After the meeting or conference, the drawings are often photographed, then cleaned up so they are legible and clear, as shown in Figure 1-5.

Dean has found that event organizers value these drawings because "the drawings have the ability to re-create the emotional impact of the event in a way that a written summary wouldn't do."

Visual notes are also an act of cocreation on the viewer's part, Dean believes: "So much of what you see on the page that's visual is what's between the lines—like comic books: frame by frame. In comics, the reader fills in between the frames."

Graphical facilitation is a natural extension of visual note taking. With graphical facilitation, the facilitator works with a group using visual techniques to help the group achieve a goal, be it to problem-solve, innovate, or arrive at a shared vision of the future.

Dean employs five tools regularly during his graphic facilitations: a mind map, a system map, a matrix, a forcefield, and a storyboard. He also likes to use visual metaphors, which empower participants in a completely new way, as shown in Figure 1-6.

These five tools help people understand how concepts are related by giving them structure. "It really opens people's thinking, by giving people easy access to other areas of their thought processes," Dean says.

Dean makes sure that, as a graphic facilitator, he is involved in the planning stages of the meeting. This allows him to decide whether to use real-world visual metaphors, archetypal symbols, or abstract shapes depending on the goals of the meeting. "If you want people to ideate with no subjectivity, to free-think, you don't want them to be tied to a real-world model," Dean explains. On the other hand, "if you want people to be more in reality and the goal is a concrete outcome, like a process map, you would want to use real-world images, even photographs," Dean says. ◆

FIGURE 1-6
The power of graphic note taking is in the artist's ability to synthesize information and present it in visual form.

In summary, visual notes enhance a meeting or conference by aiding participants' memory processes in real time. Visual notes help after the event, too, re-creating the emotional tone of the meeting.

> **[TIP]   Use Graphics to Build a Common Language**
>
> Thierry de Baillon, a consultant in France and cofounder of Socialearning, uses a deck of symbols he's created as a spark to get conversations going in his graphic facilitation sessions. Each person picks a symbol and describes what the symbol means to him or her. The goal at this stage "isn't about creativity but the perception of reality," Thierry says. "Each of us is unique—you're not seeing what your neighbor is seeing." Thierry's purpose is to identify the gap and bring about discussion of that gap. "We can then build a common language together," he says.

Slide Presentations in Visual Business

A slide presentation can be many things: a collection of images, a narrative of text, or a framework for grounding a talk. Presentations can be delivered in an arena or on a mobile phone. They can be projected, printed, shared, downloaded, saved, and liked. They can inspire, persuade, or summarize countless hours of work, research, and preparation. They can extend the life of a public event and set expectations for a future gathering.

The overwhelming volume of information that assaults us every day has made brevity an art form. It has also created a need to rely on the recommendations of people we trust for content we view and share.

Slide presentations can:

- Persuade an audience to understand and accept a premise
- Present complex data in a way that the audience will understand and internalize
- Teach people who learn and remember in different ways (auditory, visual, etc.)

Slide presentations have become increasingly important in business due to changes in human behavior brought about by technology. The next section explores two of these changes: continuous partial attention (CPA) and Generation C. Unlike Gen X and Gen Y, which were generations defined by age, Gen C is defined by its "always connected, always on" behavior. The next section shows how CPA and Gen C impact business communication and move it toward the visual.

CONTINUOUS PARTIAL ATTENTION AND GENERATION C

With the proliferation of connected devices, the technical ability to stay connected is rapidly increasing. Respected venture capital firm Kleiner Perkins Caufield & Byers reported in December of 2012 a global increase of 42% in the use of smartphones, with a 50% year-over-year growth in the United States. The number of phone plan subscribers worldwide is 1,142,000,000. That's 1.142 billion people connecting to each other and to the Internet using smartphones. Even when attending a live event, people bring their tablets and laptops and especially smartphones, as shown in Figure 1-7.

According to Nielsen's Cross-Platform Report, Q4 2012, published in March 2013, people shift between multiple screens when viewing content. Indeed, the number of households who do not use a television as the primary source of viewing content has increased 2.5 times over the last six years. Nielsen calls these households "Zero TV" households. As the report states, these Zero-TV homes accounted for less than 5% of US households six years ago and have since risen nearly 2.5 times as more households have changed the way they get their content in favor of using other devices and services. These homes now have multiple devices to choose from, and many have more than one way to access content in addition to their TV sets. The number of Zero-TV homes has grown from 2,010,000 in 2007 to 5,010,000 in 2012. This is important to creators of visual online content because it is a clear indicator of a change in behavior, in which people are turning to a variety of devices to consume content.

FIGURE 1-7
Conference attendees at SXSW Interactive Festival show their phones (photo by Kris Krug).

The challenge of an "always on" culture is that by not wanting to miss anything, people are ignoring some part of everything they tune into at once. For the public speaker, this means you have some of your audience's attention, but not all of it. Your talk is competing with the outside activities of the networks of every person in your audience who has a smartphone or Internet-connected device.

This always-on, always-connected behavior is what Linda Stone coined *continuous partial attention* (CPA): the behavior of paying simultaneous attention to a number of sources of incoming information, but at a superficial level. Not the same as *multitasking*, which is the motivation to be more productive, CPA occurs when someone wants to be always on—to be, as Linda puts it, "a live node on the network; always on, anywhere, anytime, anyplace behavior."

Generation C is a recently identified demographic, first named by Nielsen when it discovered a decrease in the number of households that were watching TV. Gen C cares about connection and content, and about content's creation and curation. For anyone or any organization trying to capture the attention of Generation C, the pressure is on to create compelling content and make it available so that people can connect with it.

Unlike previous labels of Baby Boomers or Generations X and Y, Generation C is not defined by its age. Instead, members of Gen C are identified by their behavior, the always-on lifestyle that Linda Stone identified 15 years ago. Members of Generation C know how to find what they want online and can seamlessly switch from one device or online platform to another. Gen C is a lifestyle, a group of behaviors that has come from the 24/7 availability of content and the devices that deliver it.

THE CHALLENGE FOR PRESENTERS

Because today's audience is engaged in continuous partial attention, presenters must put in extra effort to compete for the mindshare of a distracted audience. One way to win more audience attention is to include engaging visual slides with your presentation and show them intermittently instead of in parallel with your talk.

Think of your slideshow as adding percussive punctuation to a talk instead of performing a continuous accompaniment. A speaker might talk for several minutes or more without showing a visual image on the screen. Then, in order to reinforce a point or introduce a new point, the presenter shows a slide or video. In this case, the presenter uses the visual media to punctuate the talk, breaking it up, adding interest and variety. This is a very different style from the traditional use of a slideshow—running in parallel to the spoken presentation.

Some presenters, such as Baratunde Thurston, include video as well as still images in their keynote speeches. Baratunde moves from his spoken delivery to slides to video and back again as his talk progresses. The multimedia in his presentation is not running in the background; it is front and center and plays an equal role to his speaking. Visual presentations give the audience a reason to stay engaged with a live speaker. A slidedeck or video gives the audience a reason to watch, not just listen and possibly tune out.

STORYTELLING MAKES MENTORS OF PRESENTERS

In her 2010 TEDxEast talk "You Can Change the World," Nancy Duarte asserts that the presenter of an idea is not that idea's hero. To reach and persuade an audience, the presenter shouldn't be the star of the show. Just as in the classic myth or story structure, which begins with a likeable hero, a new structure has emerged. In this new structure, a problem or challenge arises and the audience-hero must confront it and battle it. There is a hesitation until the mentor-presenter arrives to help move the audience-hero to overcome the problem or challenge and reach a better world.

"The presenter isn't the hero; the audience is the hero of our idea," Duarte says. "The role of the presenter is to be the mentor." The presenter is not Luke Skywalker, the hero in George Lucas's *Star Wars* saga. Rather, the presenter is Yoda, Luke's mentor. Presenters help the audience "move from an ordinary thing into your special idea," Duarte says. "That's the power of story."

Storytelling and visual presentations keep the audience's attention and move them to action.

ACCESS DATA TO CREATE VISUALIZATIONS

Just as powerful stories make better presentations, so, too, do illustrated slideshows. Illustrated slides use visual illustrations rather than words in the slidedecks. The visual illustrations take the place of the old-style, teleprompter-type slides that just had a few bullet points.

Using illustrations rather than words in slides changes the audience's expectations of what a public speaker will provide. The expectations of preparation, supporting visuals, and overall delivery are higher. The audience is counting on receiving an engaging, interactive experience.

Along with the challenges of keeping up with the various devices on which a presentation might be viewed comes an opportunity to create more engaging visuals. Instead of relying on the graphs and charts provided by

Microsoft Excel, content creators are now finding ways to use an *application programming interface* (API) to import data into a graphic design software, as Paul Lamere of The Echo Nest demonstrates in Figure 1-8.

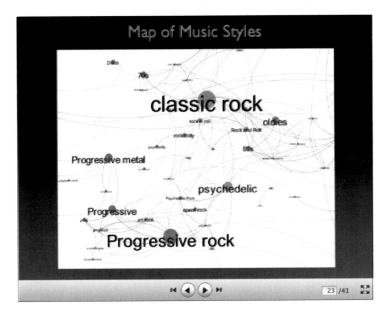

The IBM project Many Eyes is an application that turns your data into graphics, and it is free and available to everyone. Many Eyes allows pure data in either text or table format to be uploaded and processed into multiple visualization formats. You can translate anything from sales figures to scientific datasets into a visualization, with a variety of graphics to choose from and recommendations based on the desired message of the data.

Many Eyes was created by Fernanda Viégas and Martin Wattenberg, who now lead Google's Big Picture visualization research group in Cambridge, Massachusetts. Fernanda and Martin give two pieces of advice to presenters who are representing data with graphic art:

- Defy the conventional wisdom of starting with a question. Instead, explore the way the data is portrayed in imagery and discover where it takes you.
- Use a dataset that is important, and that you care about. Stay true to the data so that it will be useful.

The potential for nondesigners to communicate their message with beautiful images has never been greater. The presentation software company Haiku Deck is one company that is running with this opportunity (see the "Real-World Example" sidebar on Adam Tratt).

Adam Tratt, Haiku Deck

One of the most recent influencers in the presentation design world is a company called Haiku Deck. Not a design agency, Haiku Deck instead provides presentation software in the form of beautifully designed templates that let content creators, who are not skilled designers, add highly designed slides to their content.

Cofounder Adam Tratt says that the company was formed to solve the cofounders' own problem. Their original company was a startup that needed memorable presentations for its sales and investor pitch decks. Adam, formerly a product manager at Microsoft, recognized that a functional knowledge of PowerPoint wasn't enough to create compelling presentations. "There is a challenge when a presenter wants a creative slideshow, but does not have the design skill or a design department," Adam says.

As Adam talked to people in the business environment about their presentation design process, the responses were similar: "I know how to use those tools. I do not love using those tools." This led to the creation of Haiku Deck, shown in Figure 1-9.

Haiku Deck is a simple iPad application that allows you to create a beautiful, compelling slideshow with little to no design expertise.

Adam believes strongly in the power of storytelling. This, along with social sharing and the increased ability of devices to display visual content beautifully, has fueled an evolution of the slideshow. Adam also credits the "Instagram effect," the idea that compelling images can be created quickly and easily, for creating an expectation among viewers that beautiful photographs should be included in presentations.

Adam compares sharing a presentation to presenting a gift. It should feel good. So, with a small collection of design templates, Haiku Deck launched. Haiku Deck is integrated with SlideShare so that a presentation created with Haiku Deck can be uploaded to a SlideShare user's channel. ◆

FIGURE 1-9
Haiku Deck provides presentation templates for nondesigners.

The New World of Social Sharing

Traditionally, the bullet-point-riddled, text-saturated slides of the past were accepted with resignation by audiences who didn't know better. People were exposed to slidedecks for only the talks and live events that they attended. With the advent of SlideShare, suddenly people were able to view slide-shows from people and events they didn't know, much less participate in.

Google is not the only show in town now for getting your content noticed. *Social sharing*, the posting and "liking" of content from one user to another, is an organic recommendation engine driven by people whom you have chosen to include in your social networks. People are now designing content that is designed to be shared. Not only has the viewing been disbursed across a spectrum of devices, but the selection of content that comes your way is also selected and distributed as a democratic process. Om Malik, the founder and senior writer for GigaOm, calls this phenomenon the "democratization of distribution." Social sharing allows content to be transported to audiences that were previously unreachable.

The power of social sharing created the need for the SlideShare platform of presentation content. As it evolved, SlideShare empowered presenters to reach a worldwide audience. It also empowered viewers to share, like, and even embed presentations on their own websites. Curation of slidedecks has emerged as subject matter experts and influencers give their votes of approval with shares, likes, and embeds. Thoughtful editorial curators have tremendous power in whom and what they select to publish.

The following chapters explore the ways that you can get your content noticed and shared by curators, as well as potential customers and clients of your business.

Summary Tips

▶ Use images to explain complex material, because images are easier to understand and are less intimidating.

▶ Experiment with ways in which you can display data sets visually, because people can spot patterns and trends in pictures more easily than in numbers or words.

▶ When collaborating in a group, suggest that people sketch out ideas. The quality of the drawing is not important (in fact, rougher sketches invite more discussion).

▶ Sketch out ideas using a tool like Alex Osterwalder's Business Model Canvas in order to decrease the cognitive load people have to carry.

▶ Engage a visual notetaker to document the key ideas in a meeting or conference. Visual notes often capture more of the emotional tone than words do.

▶ Use images in your presentations to attract your audience's attention, particularly the always-on Generation C members in your audience.

▶ Use apps like Haiku Deck to create more visually compelling slides, particularly if you're not a designer.

Getting Started

It's easy to get started with SlideShare. You can set up a free account in a few minutes or go PRO to receive additional benefits. The individuals and organizations that use their free accounts on SlideShare constitute the majority of users. They are the foundation of the huge community platform and are critically important to SlideShare's growth and the wide variety of content it makes available.

PRO accounts are available for a monthly fee (with a discount for paying a year at a time), and they give you more benefits. There are three levels of PRO accounts, plus the ability to purchase a "network" that is customized for each organization. We'll explain more about the benefits of PRO accounts later in the chapter, but for now, let's get started!

Create a SlideShare Account

All new members of the SlideShare community begin by signing up for an account with an email address (see Figure 2-1). You can also choose to connect via your LinkedIn or Facebook accounts. This is advisable if you are creating your own personal SlideShare account, but not if you are creating an account for a company.

The advantage of connecting through LinkedIn or Facebook, besides not having to create another password, is that SlideShare will automatically suggest people to follow based on your LinkedIn or Facebook connections. This is a quick way to jumpstart your SlideShare community.

If you decide not to connect via LinkedIn or Facebook, simply enter a username and password and off you go.

Think carefully about your username, especially if you are signing up for your company or organization. You can never change the username for the account, even if your contact email changes over time. It's a good idea to use your name or your company name exactly as it appears in your other social networks and marketing communications, because doing so makes it easier for people to find you on SlideShare.

FIGURE 2-1
Create a SlideShare
account using your
email, or connect
with your LinkedIn
or Facebook
account.

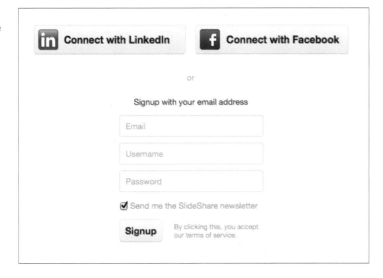

The only other question to answer before activating your account is whether you would like to receive the SlideShare newsletter, which is an editorial summary of top stories, presentations, and announcements published every two weeks. Opting into the newsletter (by checking the "Send me the SlideShare newsletter" box shown in Figure 2-1) is a good way to receive updates about SlideShare and learn about the top presentations on the site, which is useful information to help you build top-ranked presentations of your own.

Check your email and verify that, yes, you were the one who signed up for the account. SlideShare automatically logs you in, and you're ready to create your profile.

Create Your Profile

FIGURE 2-2
All of your account
options are
available from the
drop-down menu
on any SlideShare
page.

From the upper-right corner of the SlideShare screen, click on the arrow to view your account menu (see Figure 2-2).

From this menu, you can access your uploaded files, change your profile page, search the support forums, and log out. PRO users can access analytics and the full PRO dashboard as well. PRO accounts and their advantages are covered in more detail later in this chapter.

ADD YOUR PROFILE PICTURE

Choose a photo of yourself or your company's logo to display on your SlideShare profile. As the upload screen recommends in Figure 2-3, use a square image that is 96 × 96 pixels for best results.

FIGURE 2-3
Upload a photo or image that is 96 x 96 pixels and no larger than 500 KB.

If you are creating an individual account, you might want to use the same picture you've used on your other social networking sites. This will help people recognize you immediately and strengthen your personal brand.

ADD YOUR PERSONAL INFORMATION

Your personal information helps viewers and SlideShare community members understand who you are, where you're located, and how you position yourself professionally. Fill out the personal information form (see Figure 2-4) as completely as you can. This is what will display on your SlideShare profile page.

FIGURE 2-4
Include your personal information to have a complete profile.

ADD YOUR CONTACT INFORMATION

SlideShare makes it easy for members to interact. Be sure to enter your Twitter, Facebook, and LinkedIn information (see Figure 2-5) to get new followers on those social networks.

FIGURE 2-5
You can let SlideShare members contact you directly, via email or through your social networks.

Including your social networks allows viewers to follow you and connect with you more easily across all platforms.

AUTOMATICALLY SHARE YOUR UPLOADS

If you'd like to share your presentations on LinkedIn and Facebook each time you upload a file, be sure to check the Connect options, as shown in Figure 2-6.

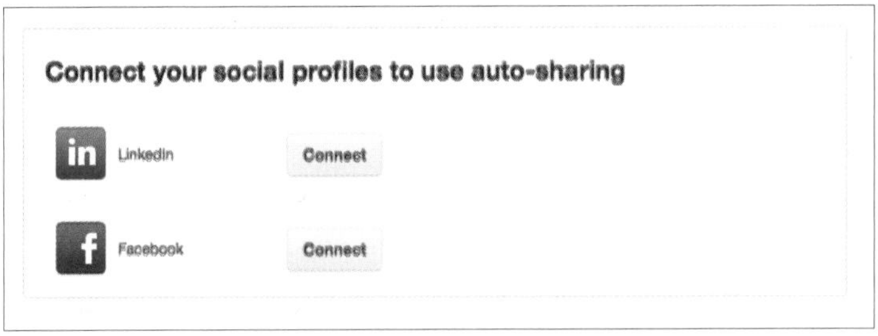

FIGURE 2-6
When you enable the autosharing option, any presentations you post on SlideShare will also automatically post to LinkedIn and Facebook each time you upload.

Social sharing is one of the fastest ways to increase traffic to your presentations.

SELECT YOUR EMAIL PREFERENCES

SlideShare notifies you when actions occur on your account. You can decide which actions you want to know about right away and indicate your choices (see Figure 2-7).

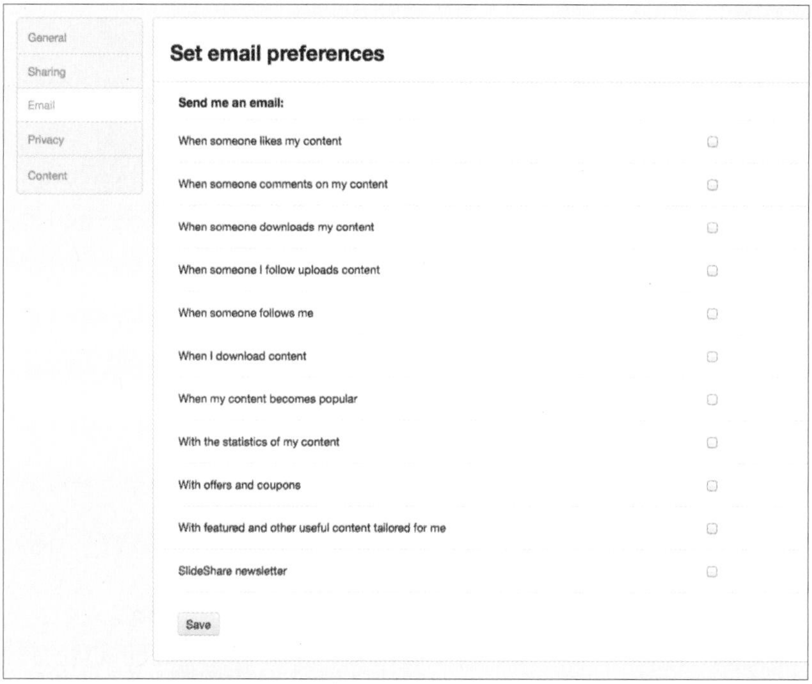

FIGURE 2-7
Select which types of information you would like to be notified of via email.

Opting to receive these notifications is useful, especially when someone likes or comments on your content. Getting these notifications means that you can interact with the person, such as by responding to her comment. People who like or follow you are probably people with whom you have mutual interests. Following them back helps you build your professional network. For a business, people who follow you might be potential or current customers. Interacting with them on SlideShare deepens the relationship.

Getting notifications when your content becomes popular gives you an early indicator of trends. It's a clear sign to use that momentum to promote that content further through other platforms—such as LinkedIn, Facebook, or Twitter—to continue spreading the word.

ADD PRIVACY SETTINGS

You can control who can send you private messages and who can share content with you. Select the options you are comfortable with (see Figure 2-8).

FIGURE 2-8
SlideShare lets
you control who
interacts with you.

CONTROL HOW VIEWERS LICENSE YOUR CONTENT

In addition to retaining all rights to your content, you can select from the six types of Creative Commons licenses (see Figure 2-9).

FIGURE 2-9
Choose whether
you'd like to
maintain a full
copyright of your
content, or one
of the Creative
Commons licenses.

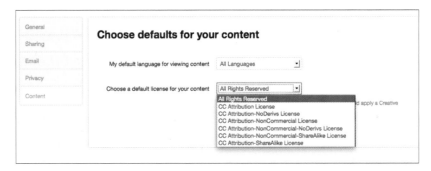

Creative Commons licenses are a free service specifying how you allow others to use your content. There are six kinds of Creative Commons licenses. Briefly, here is what each type of license means and when you should use it:

Creative Commons Attribution License

Gives others permission to distribute your work exactly as it appears, or with their own modifications or additions, as long as they credit you for the original creation. With this type of license, you grant others the right to sell your work if they choose, with no obligation or payment to you other than attributing the original content to you.

Creative Commons Attribution-ShareAlike

Gives others permission to distribute your work exactly as it appears, or with their own modifications or additions, as long as they credit you for the original creation and license their subsequent work using the identical license that you originally used.

Creative Commons Attribution-NonCommercial

Gives others permission to distribute your work exactly as it appears, or with their own modifications or additions, as long as they credit you for the original creation and do not sell the work or make it commercially available.

Creative Commons Attribution-NoDerivs

Gives others permission to distribute or even sell your work, as long as they reproduce it exactly as it appears in your original form and attribute you as the original content creator. You grant them permission to sell your content if they choose.

Creative Commons Attribution-NonCommercial-ShareAlike

Gives others permission to distribute your work (exactly or with modifications or additions), as long as they do not use it commercially and they attribute you and license their subsequent work using the identical license that you originally used.

Creative Commons Attribution-NonCommercial-NoDerivs

Gives others permission to distribute your work only if they reproduce it exactly as you originally created it, provide you attribution, and do not sell it or make it commercially available.

For more information about each of these licenses, as well as their legal codes, see *http://creativecommons.org/*.

PRO Accounts

Once you've set up your SlideShare account, you might decide to upgrade to PRO. There are three levels of PRO, plus the ability to create a SlideShare Network. Network is a customized account used by large organizations such as Dell, NASA, and IBM to decentralize publishing out to business units or thought leaders and allow their content to syndicate back to the main hub.

BENEFITS OF PRO ACCOUNTS

Here are the additional benefits you gain by upgrading to a PRO SlideShare account:

- Customize your profile design.
- Upload videos (10 for Silver, 20 for Gold, and unlimited for Platinum accounts).
- Upload larger files (300 MB presentations and up to 500 MB for videos).
- Make uploads private: create a secret URL, assign a password, and schedule a presentation to change from private to public.
- Include active hyperlinks in the description field for files.
- Remove transcripts from the slideview page (for Gold and Platinum accounts).
- Receive more detailed analytics (data increases in detail with the levels of PRO accounts).
- Track viewer activity: use SendTracker to monitor how viewers spend time on your presentations (5 presentations for Silver, 20 presentations for Gold, and unlimited for Platinum).
- Generate and collect leads using LeadShare (30 leads for Silver, 75 leads for Gold, and unlimited leads for Platinum). We'll explain how to set up LeadShare in Chapter 5.

Let's look at each of these benefits in turn.

CUSTOMIZE YOUR PROFILE

PRO accounts can control how their profile page is designed. Silver accounts can choose from a preset theme, as shown in Figure 2-10.

Gold and Platinum accounts can customize their profile page design and build their own theme using the options shown in Figure 2-11.

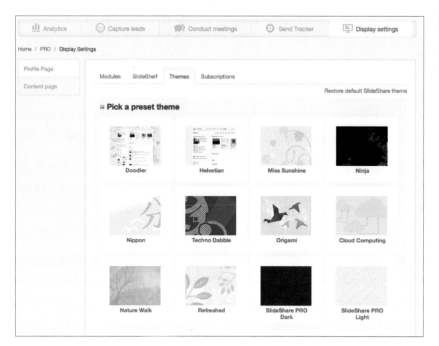

FIGURE 2-10
Silver PRO accounts allow profile customization with preset themes.

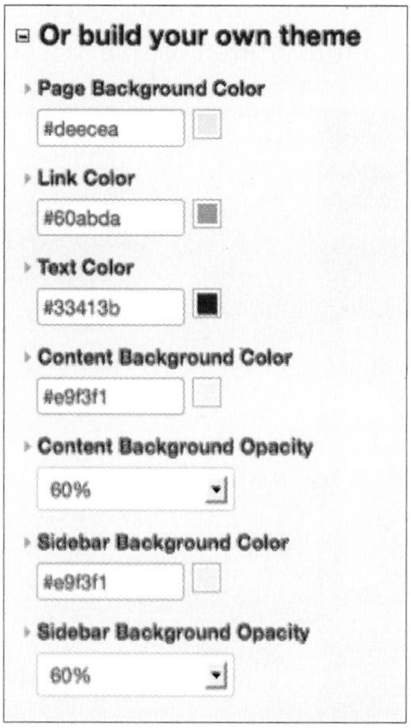

FIGURE 2-11
Gold and Platinum PRO accounts have the most design flexibility for building a theme.

UPLOAD VIDEOS AND LARGER FILES

With a PRO account, you can upload larger files, as well as videos of increasingly large size with higher account levels. Uploading videos is particularly useful if you want to show customers how to use your products or if you produce demonstrations.

Not only do Gold and Platinum accounts allow for more design flexibility with the previously mentioned HTML, but you can also upload custom images for the background, and (for Platinum accounts) the banner. Background and banner images can be in JPEG, GIF, or PNG format. Backgrounds must be 1,600 × 1,600 pixels, with a maximum size of 800 KB, while banner images must be 690 pixels wide by 100 pixels tall.

PLATINUM CUSTOM BRANDING

If you're setting up an account for a larger company and want absolute control over your branding, the Platinum account is the one to choose because it gives you more flexibility and also incorporates more social properties on your page. As a result, you establish not only a content hub but also a social media hub (with content boxes).

The first customizable piece to note is the banner image. The banner image for platinum content will play above all content within the account and is clickable. The banner image allows you to hyperlink back to your channel or even offline to a landing page, as shown in Figure 2-12.

FIGURE 2-12
The social@Ogilvy banner links back to its profile page.

In this case, the social@Ogilvy banner image links back to the profile page, which hosts the rest of the Social Ogilvy Content. Eloqua has a similar banner image, but as Figure 2-13 shows, instead of linking back to their SlideShare page, they link off SlideShare.net to their company website (*http://www.eloqua.com*).

FIGURE 2-13
Eloqua's banner links back to its company website.

These customizations add tremendous value to a SlideShare page, especially when the company has a brand strategy implemented on its content and social networks.

CREATE PRIVATE PRESENTATIONS

When you upload a presentation and want to control who views it, you can create a secret URL or set a password for it, as shown in Figure 2-14. This is particularly useful when collaborating on a work in progress, before it is made available to the public. Chapter 6 explores collaboration in more detail.

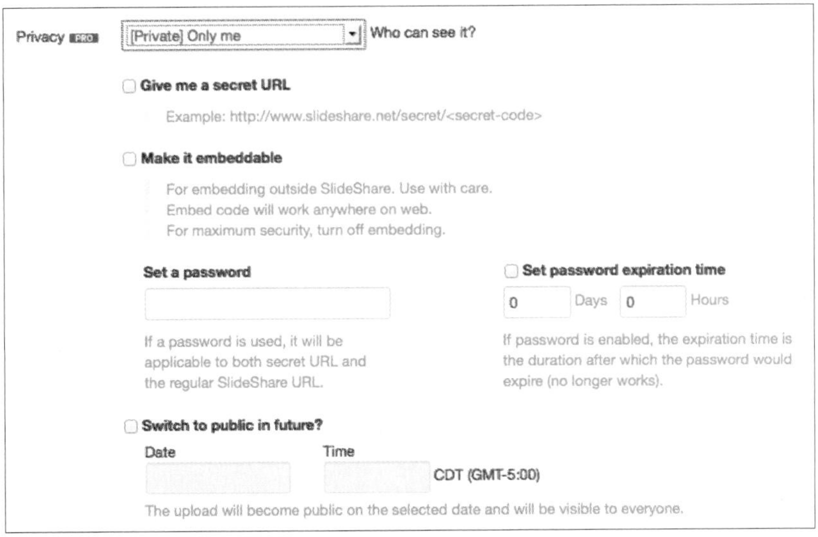

FIGURE 2-14
Control who sees
your presentation
by creating a secret
URL or setting a
password.

Private URLs and password-protected presentations are useful when you're giving a limited number of people a preview of your content—during a press embargo, for instance. They are also a great way to time the launch of content, as discussed in Chapter 8 with the example of 500 Startups.

Another benefit of PRO accounts is the ability to add active hyperlinks in the description fields for files, which means that you can put your company's URL directly in the description field. This makes it easy for your potential customers to click and visit your website directly.

The option to remove transcripts from the slideview pages means that you can restrict people from seeing your whole presentation at a glance without clicking through each slide. Restricting this at-a-glance view allows you to get metrics on exactly how many slides each viewer has seen, as discussed in the following section.

MONITOR VIEWER ACTIVITY WITH SENDTRACKER

SendTracker allows you to send new or existing content from your SlideShare account to a prospect via email. Real-time alerts let you know when the recipient has opened and clicked your email. With SendTracker, you can send content to a potential customer, see when he opened it and how he engaged with it, and gain better insights on which parts resonated most.

To set up SendTracker for a specific presentation, go to your PRO Dashboard and follow these three steps:

1. Select the presentation you'd like to track (see Figure 2-15).

FIGURE 2-15
Upload or select the presentation you want to track.

2. Add the email addresses of recipients who will receive an email from you with a custom message and a link to that presentation (see Figure 2-16).

FIGURE 2-16
Create recipients' email addresses and custom message.

3. Once the recipient opens the link to the presentation, the details about how it was viewed show up in your SendTracker (Figure 2-17).

Real-time alerts let you know when the recipient has opened and clicked your email, while analytics enable you to track how she engages with that content, as discussed in the next section.

UNDERSTAND VIEWER BEHAVIOR WITH ANALYTICS

Analytics reports provide the data about how your presentations are being viewed. This data includes details about the location of viewers, top search keywords, and your top embedded presentations. Just as analytics are used in many software programs, SlideShare analytics help you determine the effectiveness of your content. These findings inform your decisions about how to increase views and engagement with your audience.

All PRO accounts have access to SlideShare analytics. To access analytics, click on the Analytics link in the top-right drop-down menu, shown in Figure 2-18.

The Analytics Summary page displays the total amount of activity for your SlideShare content. It allows you to select a specific date range, as shown in Figure 2-19.

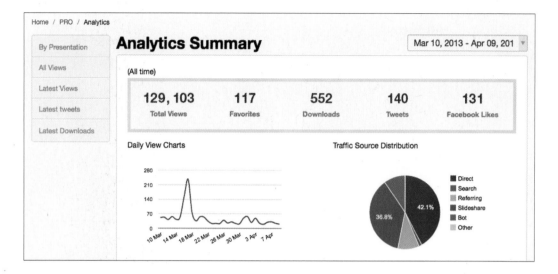

To dive more deeply into your viewers' behavior and engagement with your content, select from the options in the menu on the left side of the screen (shown in Figure 2-20). This is where you'll find data about the activity on a specific presentation.

The All Views screen displays an aggregation that includes views of presentations that are embedded on other websites plus views from the SlideShare website, as shown in Figure 2-21.

You can also find out who is tweeting your content, and what countries are viewing your content. See how many times your content has been downloaded, and by whom, on the Latest Downloads screen, shown in Figure 2-22.

Finally, with progressively higher PRO-level accounts, you can collect increasingly more leads, from 30 leads for Silver accounts, 75 leads for Gold, and unlimited leads for Platinum accounts. Chapter 5 discusses the value of this feature and how to collect leads.

FIGURE 2-19
Analytics provide actionable data about how people are viewing and interacting with your presentations.

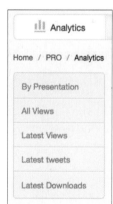

FIGURE 2-20
View detailed analytics by choosing from options in the menu on the left side of the page.

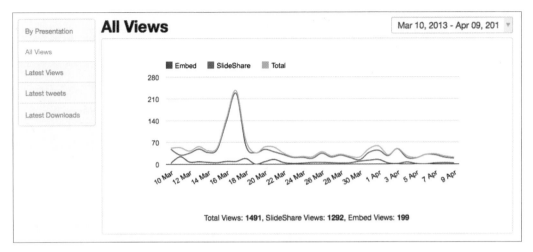

FIGURE 2-21
All Views provides aggregated analytics about presentation views.

Home / PRO / Analytics / Downloads

Users who downloaded your content

Mar 10, 2013 - Apr 09, 201

By Presentation
All Views
Latest Views
Latest tweets
Latest Downloads

	Username**	Date	Location	Presentation
1	sergio.ramiro	Apr 06, 10:31 AM	Brazil	Yahoo! Q4 2012 Quarterly Earnings
2	Amit Ranjan	Apr 03, 02:59 AM	India	Community content 2013
3	danielalexander228	Mar 22, 01:05 PM	United States	Facebook Q4 2012 Quarterly Earnings
4	Andrea Meyer	Mar 21, 04:47 PM	United States	How to catch the curator's...
5	apinhal	Mar 18, 12:06 PM	Brazil	How to catch the curator's...
6	alvarocaballero	Mar 11, 10:19 AM	Chile	Impact of climate on the winter ...

** SlideShare username, or name entered in lead collection form for LeadShare

FIGURE 2-22
Keep track of who has downloaded your content with download analytics.

Upload and Edit a Presentation

Once you've created an account on SlideShare, you'll want to upload a presentation. SlideShare supports a variety of file types, including PowerPoint, videos, and PDFs. Here's how to upload a file to your SlideShare account:

1. Log into SlideShare and click the orange Upload button (for a free account) or the blue Upload+ button (for PRO accounts) at the top of any screen (see Figure 2-23).

FIGURE 2-23
Click on the Upload button and select a file.

2. Select a file from your computer.
3. While your file is uploading, you can add information (see Figure 2-24).

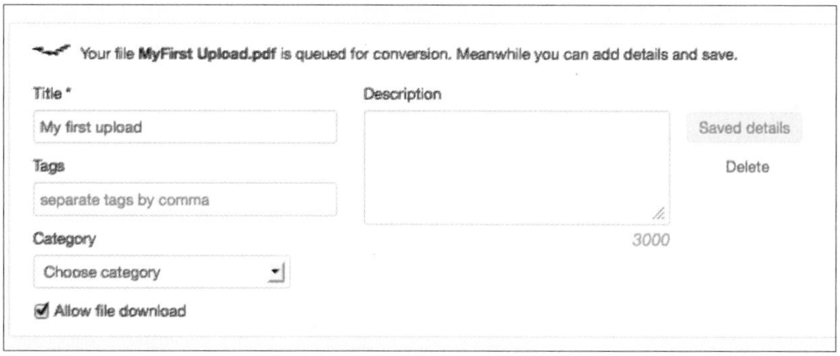

FIGURE 2-24
Add a title, description, and tags, and choose a category for your presentation.

Once your file has been published on SlideShare, a screen appears showing how it looks, along with some ways to share it on your social networks (see Figure 2-25).

You're given the embed code, in case you want to embed the file in a blog or website. Embedding your files in blog posts and on other sites is a good

FIGURE 2-25
Share your newly uploaded file on your social networks.

idea that Chapter 6 covers in more detail. You can click on the share buttons to share it via Twitter, Facebook, LinkedIn, or email.

LinkedIn allows you to share your presentation in three ways:

- Display it in your profile updates.
- Post it to a LinkedIn group.
- Send the presentation to an individual via LinkedIn mail.

You can send the email to one of your LinkedIn contacts or to someone whose email you know, even if he is not one of your direct connections (see Figure 2-26).

FIGURE 2-26
Share your presentation on LinkedIn to your profile, a group, or via email to a friend or colleague.

To see how it appears on your player page, click the My Uploads link in the account drop-down menu and select the file you'd like to see. Choose Edit Settings to change the details about your presentation, such as the title, description, and tags (see Figure 2-27).

PRIVACY FOR PRO

If you have a PRO account, you can add privacy settings to control who can view your presentation, video, or document (see Figure 2-28).

> **Privacy** `PRO` [Private] Only me ▾ Who can see it?
>
> ☐ **Give me a secret URL**
>
>   Example: http://www.slideshare.net/secret/<secret-code>
>
> ☐ **Make it embeddable**
>
>   For embedding outside SlideShare. Use with care.
>   Embed code will work anywhere on web.
>   For maximum security, turn off embedding.
>
> **Set a password**   ☐ **Set password expiration time**
>
> [   ]   0   Days   0   Hours
>
> If a password is used, it will be   If password is enabled, the expiration time is
> applicable to both secret URL and   the duration after which the password would
> the regular SlideShare URL.   expire (no longer works).
>
> ☐ **Switch to public in future?**
>
>   Date   Time
>
>   [   ]   [   ]   CDT (GMT-5:00)
>
>   The upload will become public on the selected date and will be visible to everyone.

You can set privacy either with a secret URL that is available only to the people you send it to or with a password that you create. If you'd like the password to expire so that the presentation is made public at a certain time, set the time and date for when you would like the presentation to be made public.

EMBED A YOUTUBE VIDEO IN YOUR PRESENTATION

PRO presentations can pack a bigger punch when they include an embedded YouTube video. Once you've uploaded a presentation and found a video to embed, here's how to embed it in your presentation:

1. Log into your account and select My Uploads from the drop-down menu at the top right.
2. Click Add Video on the presentation to which you want to add the YouTube video (see Figure 2-29).

3. Copy the URL of the video from YouTube.

4. Paste the URL of the video you wish to embed into the Add Video text box and select where you would like it to appear, such as after a particular slide of your presentation (see Figure 2-30).

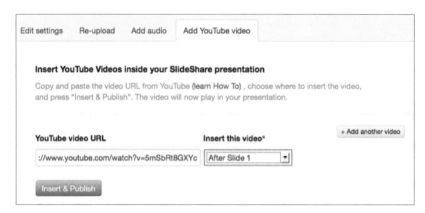

FIGURE 2-30
Copy and paste the YouTube URL into the Add Video text box.

5. Save and publish the changes.

The process of embedding a video can take up to 30 minutes, so don't worry if the video doesn't appear right away.

UPDATE A PUBLISHED FILE

If you need to update a presentation or document on SlideShare, the best method is to *replace* the existing file, rather than deleting the old one. This will allow you to save existing comments, views, tags, favorites, embeds, and its original URL. Here's how to replace an existing SlideShare using the "Re-upload" feature:

1. From the Account drop-down menu, select My Uploads.
2. Find the published file you would like to replace (see Figure 2-31).

FIGURE 2-31
Re-upload allows you to replace a file that is already on SlideShare.

3. Click Re-upload.
4. Select the file that will replace what is already on SlideShare.
5. Double-check that you are uploading the right file. If it's correct, select Upload.

The file will convert and replace the previous file, preserving your analytics, comments, and sharing activity.

You can replace presentations and documents, but not videos. The previous presentation will continue to work until the file gets replaced successfully. If replacement fails, the previous one will be intact. Once you get the confirmation that your file was successfully replaced, you might need to wait for at least 30 minutes for the new file to appear.

Embed SlideShare Presentations on LinkedIn

Presentations are powerful tools for demonstrating your knowledge, expertise, and your public speaking experience. When you display your SlideShare presentations within your LinkedIn profile, you show prospective employers, clients, customers, and your extended network that you know how to communicate with content.

This is especially true when you display a presentation that is specific to each position you have held, or conference where you have spoken.

Here's how to display your SlideShare presentations on your LinkedIn profile:

1. Log into LinkedIn and select Edit Profile.
2. To embed one or more presentations in your Background summary, click the little blue square at the top-right corner of your Summary, as shown in Figure 2-32.

FIGURE 2-32
Click on the blue square with the plus sign to add a presentation to your LinkedIn profile.

3. To include a presentation in the Experience section of your LinkedIn profile, click the blue box that appears directly below your job title.
4. In both cases (whether including the presentation in your Summary section or with a particular job in your Experience section), copy and paste the URL of your SlideShare presentation into the text box (see Figure 2-33).

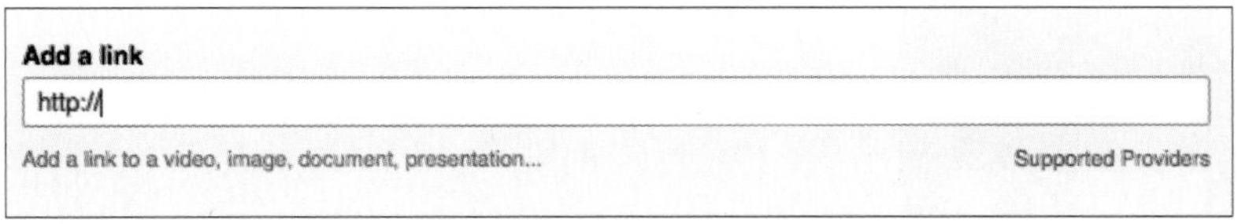

Add a link

http://

Add a link to a video, image, document, presentation...   Supported Providers

---

FIGURE 2-33
Copy and paste
your SlideShare
presentation URL
into the text box
on your LinkedIn
profile.

The presentation will then appear at the bottom of the content area. Visitors can view it without having to leave your LinkedIn profile.

Get More Views with Widgets and Badges

In addition to the social network sharing that is available when you upload a presentation, there are three free ways to promote your presentations on a website or blog.

SLIDESHARE PLAYLIST

The SlideShare Playlist widget will let you embed a custom playlist of presentations and documents on your blog or website. You can choose a feed from your tags, groups, or events. You can also choose a feed from your uploaded or favorited SlideShare content or give your feed a custom title.

This is a great way to showcase your work or the presentations from your team. It's also a great curation tool when you create a feed based on a tag, group, or event. Christian Heilmann, Web Evangelist at Mozilla in London, developed the prototype of this widget. You'll find the code (which you can copy and paste) at *http://www.slideshare.net/widgets/playlist.*

SIDEBAR WIDGET

The Sidebar widget is just like the SlideShare Playlist, except it appears as a vertical display of slideshows that can be used as a sidebar on your website or blog, as shown in Figure 2-34.

Use this widget to embed a feed of presentations and documents on your blog or website. You can select the feed from your tags, groups, or events, or from your uploaded or favorited SlideShare content.

You'll find the code at *http://www.slideshare.net/widgets/blogbadge.*

FIGURE 2-34
The Sidebar widget displays slideshows on either side of a website.

MINI BADGES

Use mini badges to provide a link from your blog or website to your SlideShare profile. They are a quick and effective way to show visitors to your website that you have presentations on SlideShare.

The badges come in a variety of shapes and sizes, ranging from 32 × 32 pixels square to a 160 × 30-pixel rectangular banner, as shown in Figure 2-35.

Select a badge and copy the embed code to your website, as shown in Figure 2-36. Each badge has its own snippet of code that you or your developer can insert into your website. All of the badges and their codes can be found at *http://www.slideshare.net/widgets/minibadge*.

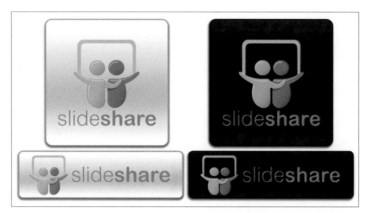

FIGURE 2-35
Badges let visitors
to your website
know that you
have content on
SlideShare.

FIGURE 2-36
Embed a SlideShare
badge on your
website.

Summary Tips

▶ Create a free SlideShare account in minutes, which you can upgrade to a PRO account to get more benefits.

▶ If you are creating a personal account, you can connect via your LinkedIn or Facebook accounts to automatically get suggestions of people to follow based on your LinkedIn or Facebook connections.

▶ Choose your username carefully. Using your name or your company name exactly as it appears in your other social networks and marketing communications will make it easier for people to find you on SlideShare.

▶ Upgrade to a PRO SlideShare account if you'd like to customize your profile design, upload videos or larger files (up to 500 MB), make some presentations private, include active hyperlinks in the description field, track detailed viewer activity, or collect leads.

▶ Compare the three levels of PRO accounts and upgrade if you need increased analytics and lead generation options.

▶ If you are a large organization, create a SlideShare Network to decentralize publishing out to business units or individual employees and syndicate their content back to your main hub.

Events and Public Speaking

They didn't come to your presentation to see you. They came to find out what you can do for them. Success means giving them a reason for taking their time, providing content that resonates, and ensuring it's clear what they are to do.

—NANCY DUARTE
Slide:ology

WHETHER YOU'RE A BUSINESS owner or a professional at a company, live events and public speaking play a key role in demonstrating your thought leadership. You can use SlideShare in all stages of event planning and execution, and even after the event, to gain more visibility.

If you're new to public speaking, and nervous at the idea of presenting to an audience, try starting small. Offer to report on an interesting topic at work, to an organization where you volunteer, or to a local professional group. Create a short slide presentation to accompany your talk. This gives you great practice in creating slides and practicing your talk while moving through the slides.

As you become more comfortable over time, try creating longer presentations. There are many informal groups where you can practice speaking using slides. From Tweetups (where like-minded Twitter users gather at an agreed-upon place and time) to Toastmasters (a nonprofit organization focused on helping you develop public speaking and leadership skills through practice and feedback), you'll find local opportunities to practice.

The proliferation of groups organized via online services like Meetup.com and Eventbrite provides further topics and potential audiences. Take heart: no one jumped onto the TED or the World Economic Forum stage as her first public speaking experience. A few slides that accompany a 10-minute talk is a great milestone when you're just starting out. Before you know it, you'll be getting requests for appearances and meeting people you thought were out of reach.

Speaking at Industry Conferences

Industry events and trade shows bring thousands of people together every year. Being a speaker at one of these events gives you the biggest exposure to the largest number of people, whether it be for you personally or for your company.

We'll begin by looking at what you can expect as a speaker at an existing event and how using SlideShare can help you build clients and be invited to speak again. After that, we'll describe the ins and outs of hosting your own event.

As you start to give talks and presentations to local or small groups, word will quickly get out that you are an interesting and engaging presenter. The events where you're invited to present will get larger. As this happens, make sure you have all your bases covered—from the technology (bring your own power supply, a backup of your presentation, and your own clicker) to a comfort level with your talk—even if the slides are not available.

The larger the venue, the more things can go wrong, so it's critically important to be as self-contained as possible. Don't rely on the conference organizers to provide you with things you can bring yourself. Anything that will reduce uncertainty will keep your stress level under control. It's natural to be nervous before a presentation. Even the most seasoned presenters get a last-minute surge of adrenaline. There's no reason to add to any stage fright by scrambling to find a missing piece of equipment or file.

One thing that popular conference speakers know is that past performance is an indicator of future success. So they own that success and pay it forward by being prepared. Experienced speakers also know that scouts for future speaking gigs are often in the audience, so treat your presentation as a way to market yourself into future engagements. One professional who has done this with great success is Liz Ngonzi (see her "Real-World Example" sidebar).

SlideShare Across the Conference Lifespan

For organizers of events, and the speakers who present, SlideShare can be used at every stage of the conference life cycle. From research to sharing after everyone goes home, presentations are an event and speaker's social networking killer app. You can use SlideShare in all stages of event planning and execution, and even after the event, to increase your visibility.

[REAL-WORLD EXAMPLE]   # Liz Ngonzi of Amazing Taste

Liz Ngonzi, CEO of Amazing Taste LLC and an international speaker and educator, presented on a panel at South by Southwest (SXSW), an annual music, film, and interactive conference that attracts more than 20,000 registrants a year. "I demonstrated my expertise in a particular content area," Ngonzi says, describing her rationale for presenting.

Potential clients—in Ngonzi's case, organizers of tech conferences in Africa, which is Ngonzi's target area—were in the SXSW audience. "I showcased my presentations in real time by sharing a link to a couple of my slidedecks with the organizers," Ngonzi says. "They emailed me the next day and booked me for a few slots to speak in their conferences."

Let's deconstruct what Ngonzi did, so you can do it too. First, Ngonzi uploaded her presentations to SlideShare. Second, she uploaded videos that show her speaking at other events, as shown in Figure 3-1. Third, she uploaded her biography on SlideShare, so that when users access her page, they see the breadth of her offerings. Finally, she integrated most of her SlideShare content into her own website, which gives visitors to her site a dynamic, multimedia experience.

When Ngonzi wants to be a speaker at a particular conference, she refers the conference organizers to her SlideShare page. This way, the conference organizers can preview her content and see her live-speaking style by watching her videos.

As an individual or a representative for your company, you can do the same. Take an existing presentation (or create a new one) and upload it to your SlideShare channel. Upload videos that show you in action. Tag this content using keywords targeted to your industry and topic. Use SlideShare to find events in similar subject matter areas and contact the event organizers, sending them a link to your SlideShare page and a brief description of why you'd be an excellent speaker for their event. ◆

FIGURE 3-1
Use videos along with slideshow presentations to give conference organizers a preview of your speaking ability.

[**REAL-WORLD EXAMPLE**] Justin Fogarty of Ariba

 Let's look at how one company, Ariba, uses Slideshare across the full lifespan of its events. Ariba is a business-to-business (B2B) commerce solutions provider that holds an annual conference, Ariba LIVE, for its customers and prospects. How does Ariba use SlideShare throughout the conference process?

First, Ariba uses SlideShare prior to the event, posting content to SlideShare before the conference even starts. "We want to get people excited about the event and help them navigate it to figure out where they want to be," explains Justin Fogarty, Ariba's social media manager. In 2011, Ariba posted its Ariba LIVE materials two weeks before the conference started. In 2012, it decided to post the content even sooner. "We [wanted] to make more noise this time," Fogarty says. From Ariba LIVE 2011's success, Fogarty knew that users were viewing content, sharing it, and even engaging in dialogue with speakers before the event.

Following those positive results, Ariba decided to upgrade to a SlideShare custom-branded channel, which gave Ariba an opportunity to generate sales leads. By posting all of its conference content on its SlideShare channel instead of allowing users to download presentations, Ariba's account management, customer success, and sales teams could track how users were consuming the information and visualize how it was spreading internally among customers or sales prospects.

With the custom channel, Ariba used SlideShare to support regional events (such as those held in Nashville or London) in addition to its primary annual conference. It also uploaded white papers (called "Ariba Knowledge Nuggets") and case studies. Early results were already promising: content on the Ariba channel had been viewed 40,000 times and generated 400 sales leads.

During the conference, Ariba attendees could view slides on their mobile phones to decide which of the numerous concurrent sessions to attend. Most important, attendees could access and share content with peers while the events were happening. "I like SlideShare's simplicity—you give people a URL, and they can view it on their web browser or mobile device," Fogarty says.

After the conference, users could watch a session on the Ariba Presentation Channel, because Ariba synchronized audio and video with the slidedecks. "The sharing and embedding is fantastic," Fogarty adds. "Also, the search engine optimization ability is hugely important, because now people can find content that might otherwise be buried on a corporate portal."

When it comes to the future of corporate events, Fogarty believes that social and mobile are intertwined. "You've got to help people find what they need quickly and share it quickly," he says. "With social and mobile content, you can really have a terrific event." ◆

ORGANIZERS: RESEARCH PROGRAM TOPICS

When you begin to plan a conference, one of the first things to think about early on is the *program*. There are many ways to mix and match program elements to provide an interesting and engaging event. You can have your audience stay in the same place and have the speakers change locations. Or you can host a classroom-style format, in which the audience changes rooms after each session. Remember, the fewer people in motion, the more likely your event will stay on schedule.

You can also decide between panels and individual speakers. Individual speakers can provide depth on a topic, while panels can provide breadth and multiple views. Many events combine all of these options. Publish your program ahead of your event so potential attendees can see what to expect, as the Association of Environmental Professionals does in Figure 3-2.

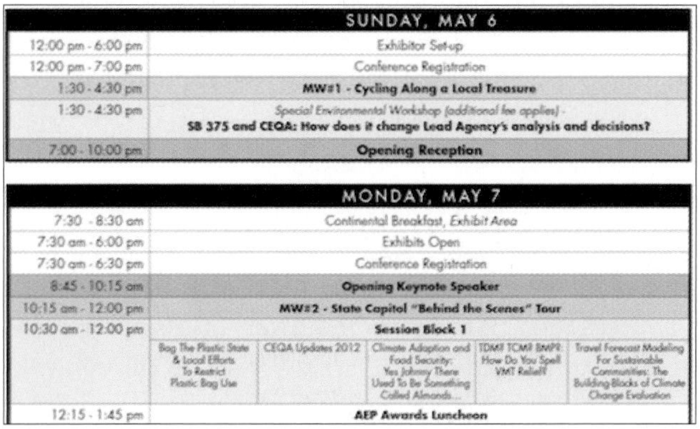

SUNDAY, MAY 6					
12:00 pm - 6:00 pm	Exhibitor Set-up				
12:00 pm - 7:00 pm	Conference Registration				
1:30 - 4:30 pm	**MW#1 - Cycling Along a Local Treasure**				
1:30 - 4:30 pm	*Special Environmental Workshop (additional fee applies)* - **SB 375 and CEQA: How does it change Lead Agency's analysis and decisions?**				
7:00 - 10:00 pm	**Opening Reception**				
MONDAY, MAY 7					
7:30 - 8:30 am	Continental Breakfast, *Exhibit Area*				
7:30 am - 6:00 pm	Exhibits Open				
7:30 am - 6:30 pm	Conference Registration				
8:45 - 10:15 am	**Opening Keynote Speaker**				
10:15 am - 12:00 pm	**MW#2 - State Capitol "Behind the Scenes" Tour**				
10:30 am - 12:00 pm	**Session Block 1**				
	Bag The Plastic State & Local Efforts To Restrict Plastic Bag Use	CEQA Updates 2012	Climate Adaption and Food Security: Yes Johnny There Used To Be Something Called Almonds...	TDM? TCM? BMP?: How Do You Spell VMT Relief?	Travel Forecast Modeling For Sustainable Communities: The Building Blocks of Climate Change Evaluation
12:15 - 1:45 pm	**AEP Awards Luncheon**				

FIGURE 3-2
Post the event schedule in a slidedeck to give potential attendees a preview.

Once you have decided upon a theme for your conference, start brainstorming topics for speakers to present. Then think of a few ideas that cross into your main theme, but aren't in the mainstream of what people are talking and writing about. Balance between content that is expected and unexpected. Including new, edgy, or unexpected topics and speakers helps you get press coverage and maintains attendees' interest in attending future events.

For example, if you're organizing an event about patient care, attendees will expect sessions that address topics like improvements in healthcare. Why not include a session that addresses the use of art and design to communicate patient needs?

Some events are held in multiple cities, combining a core group of repeat speakers plus new names to keep the event fresh—for example, An Event Apart, WebVisions, and Social Media for Nonprofits. The advantage for repeat speakers is the opportunity to grow a national audience, and to evolve the presentation material based on audience feedback. The advantages for organizers are threefold:

- Repeating the format reduces planning time.
- The speakers are known and test-driven.
- The reach is increased as the event builds its brand over time and broadens its base with new locations.

Keeping a broad focus, with repeat speakers, allows the event brand to grow while reducing the risk involved with a new crop of speakers each time. Make the event unique with location-specific expert speakers and some extra activities. For example, WebVisions introduces the heart of each host city's design community by offering a half-day of studio tours.

ORGANIZERS: FIND SPEAKERS

Use SlideShare to plan future programs and select speakers. For example, the Nonprofit Technology Network (NTEN) uses SlideShare to view past presentations from potential speakers as part of its selection process.

Start by searching on SlideShare using the topics you are considering in your program. For example, if you're planning an event about open government, search SlideShare for "open government," "open gov," "transparency," "public sector," and any other keywords that come to mind. You can filter the search by relevance, timeframe of upload, and type of file. Your results will probably include names you are familiar with, because the search results are displayed in order based on number of views. You will also most likely see a new name that is worth checking out. A fresh voice is always welcome at an event. Take a look at the person's presentation, learn more about him from his SlideShare profile, and click through to his website, LinkedIn profile, and social networks.

Conference planners can also use the website Lanyard.com to find speakers based on their SlideShare presentation decks. Lanyard allows you to filter search results based on topic, year, place, and person speaking, as shown in Figure 3-3.

You can track an event to see who will be speaking. SlideShare actually refers to Lanyard in spotlighting events on the SlideShare home page. When you're looking for speakers, use Lanyard.com to complement your searches on SlideShare.

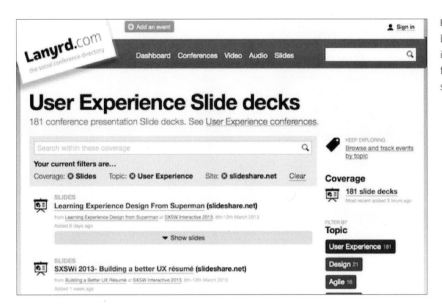

SPEAKERS: FIND YOUR MARKET

As a part of your public speaking strategy, you can use SlideShare to find out which events feature presentations in your area of expertise. Check the event's website for a "Call for Speakers" page. Then pitch your presentation to the conference organizer. Be creative: look for an industry angle for your talk.

For example, if you speak about the importance of collaboration, find a niche twist to make it relevant to multiple kinds of audiences, like "Collaboration for Managers" or "Collaboration for Customer Service Reps," or to different industries by offering talks on "Collaboration in Pharma" or "Collaboration in the Automotive Industry." If you're a company representative who speaks at your customer's conferences, expand your sphere by looking at your customers' customers to see about speaking at their events.

ORGANIZERS: PREPARE YOUR TEAM

You've already seen how uploading event information helps publicize it to attendees, but you can also use SlideShare to organize and prepare speakers and staff.

Upload speaker guidelines to SlideShare, explaining what you expect speakers to do. In particular, if the event is providing the speaker's laptop, be sure that every speaker knows what presentation software the conference supports. Also, tell speakers to bring their presentation on a thumb drive (or two) and have it already uploaded to SlideShare as a backup.

Upload a staff and volunteer orientation slideshow. As an organizer, you're expected to know everything that's happening before, during, and after your event. Of course, that's not possible, which is why it's worth being selective about your support team—even the volunteers, who are your ears to the ground and feet on the floor.

[TIP]   Help Your Staff Be Effective

To help your staff be effective, record a volunteer orientation presentation and have it available on SlideShare. Explain how the event will run and what roles your staff and volunteers will be playing. Make expectations clear, and include links to the event's online schedule.

There should be an inherent sense of urgency in every event team member's psyche. Once the event starts, there is only one speed: fast. Fix it, find it, find her, stop him, get it, go go go. It doesn't stop until you collapse into a comfortable chair at the wrap party. The time you invest in preparing and communicating with your event team will come back to you in reduced stress and increased potential for success.

Publicize Your Event with Presentations

Event organizers know that promotion for the next event begins as soon as their current event wraps up. All of the presentations, blog posts, and socially shared content serve as marketing and promotion for the next conference. Savvy organizers don't let this content slip away. Instead, they make sure that it is shared with attendees as well as potential attendees who may have missed the event. This activity builds momentum and strengthens the brand of the event.

Create a slidedeck that describes your event and links to the online registration page, as Chris Hamilton of salestipaday.com has done for his Strategies for Marketing Boot Camp, shown in Figure 3-4.

When you upload it to SlideShare, include event details in the description field, and be sure to add keywords. Encourage viewers to like and share the event promotion slidedeck with their social networks.

FIGURE 3-4
Generate interest
in your event with
an informational
slidedeck.

ORGANIZERS: ATTRACT NEW ATTENDEES

The American Society of Nephrology (ASN) holds an annual conference. "Naturally, nephrologists and nephrology nurses attend the conference," says Catherine Dold, whom the ASN hired as the social media strategist for the conference. "But the ASN also wanted to attract medical students to the conference."

There's a shortage of doctors specializing in nephrology just at a time when demand for nephrologists is rising and is projected to continue rising due to the prevalence of diabetes in the US. "We used SlideShare to get the word out to medical students," Dold says. Students using the Web for their research—combined with SlideShare's high rankings on Google searches— meant that students could more easily find out about the conference.

[**REAL-WORLD EXAMPLE**] Nonprofit Technology Enterprise
Network (NTEN)

The Nonprofit Technology Enterprise Network (NTEN) is a membership organization that works with the community of technologists who serve nonprofits. Over the years, NTEN has learned that people find out about its annual conference, the Nonprofit Technology Conference (NTC), through SlideShare.

"We will get folks interested in the NTC and NTEN because they have stumbled across a presentation from the conference on SlideShare," writes NTEN Program Director

Anna Richter in Melanie Mathos and Chad Norman's book *101 Social Media Tactics for NonProfits* (Wiley). Similarly, NTEN Executive Director Holly Ross says, "We can tell anecdotally that people are finding out more about the show. It helps us reach a new audience. It's not just a promotional message; it's real content. So when we look at our website analytics of the people who come from SlideShare, we find that they spend more time on our site."

NTEN posts the presentation slides from its NTC conferences each year. In 2010, NTEN uploaded 59 conference slideshows, and in 2011, it uploaded 71 slideshows.

NTEN asks its speakers to upload their slides to SlideShare using the event's *hashtag* (a word used in a tweet to denote a topic on Twitter—see the section "Organizers: Use Hashtags" later in this chapter for more details), which is consistent across NTC but specific to each year.

Having the presentations in one place makes it possible to share information from NTC with members who could not attend, and to maintain momentum throughout the year. ◆

SPEAKERS: BE PREPARED

As a speaker, let the organizer know well in advance if you have any special sound or lighting requirements. Organizers will remember (and tell other organizers!) which speakers are prepared and proactive and which are difficult or technically unprepared. As a speaker, if you make the organizers' jobs easy, they will remember and likely invite you to speak at future events.

When you speak at a professional event, remember it's not just your presentation that counts. Here are five ways to be the speaker that every event organizer wants to invite back:

Understand the event's community

Get to know your audience ahead of the event. Spend some time with them (online or in person), and make sure you're current with the most relevant topics of discussion or debate. This will especially help if you choose to have a question-and-answer session. Find out who the other speakers are, and publicly reach out to them. This will help build momentum and camaraderie in advance of the event.

Promote the event

A speaker's own following or readership is a great source of potential attendees for a conference. Organizers are aware of this and will notice when you actively promote the event to your community. Get the word out on your blog, shared calendars, message boards, and social networks.

Be dependable

Organizers choose speakers who show up on time, have all their materials, are prepared for A/V mishaps, and can adapt to last-minute changes. Your reputation matters. Many speakers don't realize it, but conference organizers of different events compare notes and talk among themselves to share their experiences working with speakers, on and off the stage.

Expect the unexpected

When it comes to professional events, Murphy's Law prevails. Don't assume there will be a dependable Internet connection. If you plan on presenting a "live demo," make sure you have backup screenshots handy, in case the Internet connection isn't as speedy or stable as you need.

Participate in the event

Don't just fly in, speak, and fly out. It doesn't matter how busy you are; the event is your customer, and the audience is your extended community. Be approachable and make time to engage with attendees in the halls, in other sessions, at lunch. Be willing to do an impromptu podcast, and be a good sport about having your picture taken with attendees. An engaged, supportive speaker is like an honored guest: if you are genuine and gracious, you will surely be invited back.

Be forewarned that your presentation might be videotaped, so keep in mind that what is said in your session, including before and after your formal presentation, will likely be shared with the world. This is important when you are presenting new information from your employer or client. Get prior approval in writing, and when in doubt, leave it out.

Most public conferences expect that you'll share your slidedeck. With the immediate buzz that's created on social networks during an event, the opportunity to share should be welcomed. If the content of your presentation is proprietary or the intellectual property is part of your value proposition as a speaker and you don't want it shared, be sure to tell the organizer prior to the event.

Large conferences will often ask you to send your slidedeck in advance of the actual event. Organizers are looking for any potential technical glitches, and many times, the event slidedecks are posted on the event SlideShare channel immediately following the event. The event may also want to add a cover slide template to the beginning of all the presentations to give them consistent branding. The organizers may send the cover slide to you, or add it to the presentation you send them. Ask the organizer if you can stylize the cover slide a bit, so it doesn't look identical to the other presentations.

Having the event upload your presentation to their channel is an advantage for you as a speaker, because you get the added exposure from the event's SlideShare channel in addition to exposure on your own individual channel.

ORGANIZERS: USE HASHTAGS

One of the first things to do in in an event's promotion plan is create a Twitter ID and hashtag for the event, and add the Follow icon along with the event's hashtag on the event website. As mentioned previously, a hashtag is simply a word or abbreviation preceded by the pound sign (#)—such as #SlideShare or #innovation or #NTEN13—used to denote a particular topic within a tweet.

If the event repeats in multiple locations or dates, use a hashtag that specifies the location or year. For example, WebVisions New York City becomes hashtag #WVNYC, or the event organizers can be even more specific, using #WVNYC12 to include the year. The trade-off is that the longer the hashtag, the less room there is for content in the tweet. Balance uniqueness with brevity.

Communicate the designated hashtag to your speakers. Encourage them to include it in their own tweets and on their contact information slide in order to build buzz. Hashtags also provide an easy way for people to find and hopefully curate presentations from your event.

SPEAKERS: BENEFIT FROM SHARING CONTENT

With the use of social media during live events comes the instant sharing of wise words, photographs, opinions, praise, and criticism. Organizers and presenters are not only delivering information to the people in the room; they're delivering to each of their social networks.

The in-person attendees of the event are your "studio audience." The reach of your presentation stretches much further than the conference room, in both distance and time. You and your presentation will be pinned on Pinterest, played on YouTube, shared on Instagram, and tweeted till the cows come home.

SPEAKERS: PAY IT FORWARD

If the event has a SlideShare account dedicated to the event, and you upload to your own SlideShare account, you'll receive views from both accounts' social networks. Encourage audience members to embed your slideshow on their blogs.

You can do this in a blog post about your topic, a review of your presentation, or a deeper exploration of the topic. This promotes community around the subject matter, raises the event's (and your) visibility, and helps to establish you as a subject matter expert. Sharing is good.

[**PRESENT YOURSELF TIP**] Twitter and Your Slideshow Can Work Together

Make it easy for Twitter users in the room to share your knowledge and contact info. Most events have a hashtag to identify the event on Twitter, like #PYconf. Many events include specific Twitter hashtags for each session. Include both the session and event hashtags, along with your Twitter ID, in your opening and closing slides.

In your slidedeck, come up with a few quotable words of wisdom. Make sure they are less than the total of 140 characters, minus the event hashtag and "via @your Twitter ID."

For example, create a slide (see Figure 3-5) with this quote in large font, leaving enough room for the

audience tweeters to add your Twitter ID and the event hashtag (bonus points for including cc@eventtwitterid):

> *Ask not what your social network can do for you, but what you can do for your social network.*

This quotable line contains 92 characters (with spaces), which makes it easily tweetable, especially since the audience can quote the wording right from your slide on the big screen.

The audience will add your Twitter ID plus the hashtag for the conference. The final tweet shared by your audience members will look like Figure 3-6: "RT @zsazsa: Ask not what your social network can do for you, but what you can do for your social network. #PYconf".

The tweet contains 101 characters + 11 = 112 characters with spaces. A quote with fewer than 120 characters leaves plenty of room for your audience members' tweets to be retweeted, exponentially increasing the reach of your original statement. ◆

Ask not what your social network can do for you, but what you can do for your social network. #PYconf

39 **Tweet**

FIGURE 3-5
Create a tweetable quotation and include it in your presentation.

RT @zsazsa: Ask not what your social network can do for you, but what you can do for your social network. #PYconf

27 **Tweet**

FIGURE 3-6
Leave enough characters for audience members to retweet.

ORGANIZERS: PROMOTE EVENTS

Create a SlideShare account for the event, or if there is more than one location or date, create a SlideShare network. Let speakers know that you'll be uploading their slidedecks to the event account, and encourage them to upload to their own SlideShare accounts as well.

Tag the presentations with keywords about the event, topic, and speaker, as well as the text version of the event hashtag. If you have any press or media members in attendance, let them know that slidedecks will be available to embed in articles they may write reviewing the event.

Discussion Panels

A *discussion panel* provides an interesting—and often controversial—conversation on a particular topic among several subject matter experts. The panel consists of a moderator and, ideally, no more than four additional panelists. In the case of larger events, the panelists may live in different locations and may not have met in person until the event.

The event organizer may select the panelists or, just as often, the panel moderator has enough knowledge, experience, and relationships with experts to select the members of the panel. In either case, it is the moderator's responsibility to make sure that each panelist has the event and venue information, is aware of the expectations and experience level of the audience, and knows the time limits and format of the panel.

Just as with presentations delivered by individual speakers, panel discussions have a beginning, middle, and end. Unless the panelists are famous celebrities, most audience members don't attend panel presentations to watch a few experts chat aimlessly. They want content and the opportunity to ask questions. The event PopTech (Figure 3-7) brings together experts from around the world to discuss ways individuals can improve the world.

FIGURE 3-7
A panel at PopTech
provides discussion
with diverse
perspectives (photo
by Kris Krug).

Panels provide a broad overview of a topic, with subject matter experts as panelists offering a variety of perspectives. Panels are particularly effective for discussions that introduce differing points of view, or when the panelists have achieved similar goals in distinctly different ways. Conference attendees often are looking for ways to solve a problem. An effective panel discussion can provide perspective and choices for solving that problem.

A panel is not effective when it consists of several subject matter experts who all operate the same way and agree on the value or approach to the topic. The audience is smart enough to not need to hear four people say virtually the same things about the same points. Instead, assemble a diversity of speakers to provide different points of view.

ROLE OF THE PANEL MODERATOR

A well-prepared moderator will select panelists carefully. The panel format may consist of the moderator asking a series of questions, with each panelist giving his or her response. It is common practice to provide these questions to the panelists in advance, so they have time to frame thoughtful answers. The moderator will conduct a conference call or, at minimum, an email thread with all of the panelists in order to ensure that the goals of the panel session are clear.

Alternatively, each panelist may deliver a prepared mini-presentation. If a panelist plans to show a slidedeck, the moderator needs to be sure the panelist is aware of the time constraints. Moderators must also manage the panelists' time allotments during the event, if necessary. In cases where panelists have prepared presentations, the moderator needs to make sure that the room is outfitted with A/V equipment and that any other requirements for the event are met. A prepared panel uses its time efficiently, stays on topic, and provides time for a question-and-answer period.

The moderator should always introduce each of the panelists individually. She should prepare a short slidedeck with, at the minimum, a slide dedicated to each of the panelists with an image of the panelist's company or website, and contact information. The moderator may want to include a few slides that give context for the discussion, and then a closing slide that lists the entire panel with contact information.

Even though the panel moderator is knowledgeable and most likely has an opinion about the panel's topic, she needs to maintain a neutral position in order to best facilitate the discussion, keep the session moving forward, and manage the question-and-answer period. The primary responsibility of the moderator is to facilitate healthy discussion. When a moderator gets caught up in the dialogue and starts to participate, she loses control of the panel. The value of the session decreases almost immediately. If a panel devolves in this manner, it happens quickly, is noticed by the audience, and will be reflected in attendee feedback.

It's also the moderator's job to manage the question-and-answer period. The moderator selects audience members to pose questions to the panel. If an audience microphone is not available, the moderator should repeat the question, or a summary of the question, so that the entire audience can hear. This is also important if the session is being recorded, so that the future listening audience hears the question as well as the answer that follows. If there isn't enough time for Q&A, the moderator should announce to the audience that panelists will be available for questions in one of the public spaces. This is the way to quickly clear the stage after the panel session as a courtesy to the next session.

The Unconference

In an *unconference*, audience members are participants. In the original format, a discussion leader is appointed and begins to "craft a story from the expertise in the room." Typically, everyone—audience members and potential speakers alike—meet the night before the unconference. During this presession, people list the topics they'd like to hear about and the topics they could present on. Speakers and topics are matched, with voting taking place as needed to identify top-priority topics. The unconference organizer posts a giant schedule for the unconference day, with blank spots next to the timeslots and meeting rooms available. Speakers sign up to present their topic during an open timeslot. On the day of the event, audience members choose which sessions they will attend.

For example, innovation and knowledge management consultant Christian de Neef proposed an unconference following the widely attended World Innovation Forum held annually in New York City. The World Innovation Forum is the equivalent of the World Economic Forum in Davos (but focused on innovation), with only the top experts in the world presenting, such as Harvard Business School Professor Clayton Christensen and Fortune 100 CEOs.

Given the handful of speakers at the World Innovation Forum but the thousands of attendees and potential speakers, de Neef saw an opportunity. De Neef lives in Belgium and conducts most of his business in Europe and the Middle East. He saw the unconference as a way to expand his network in the US. He proposed the idea through Twitter to participants of InnoChat, an innovation-related discussion that takes place on Twitter each week. De Neef invited innovation practitioners and consultants attending the World Innovation Forum to extend their stay by a day to attend the unconference and have the opportunity to present their own work to new colleagues. The event's success led to subsequent unconferences in the following years. Unconference presenters like Jose Briones then posted their slides to SlideShare to continue the discussion and share it with a wider audience.

Unconferences have branched out to include events such as Barcamps, which are shorter-format unconferences taking place over a few hours at a private room in a restaurant or bar (hence the name Barcamp). Julian Loren, a Paris- and Berkeley-based consultant, has hosted dozens of Barcamps around the country and then posts the slides to SlideShare.

Lightning Presentations

Lightning events are fast-presentation events in which each presentation is limited to a few minutes—from 5 to 18 minutes, usually—as discussed in the following examples.

PECHAKUCHA NIGHT

PechaKucha Night started in Tokyo and draws its name from the Japanese term for the sound of "chit chat." The format is simple: the speaker takes the stage with 20 slides, each displaying for 20 seconds. Creating a presentation within these constraints works best when the topic is unexpected and the images are full of surprises.

The organizational structure behind PechaKucha is nonprofit, with organizers putting together these local events in their spare time. Why participate in a PechaKucha Night? If you're just getting started as a public speaker, or you want to explore speaking on a new topic, PechaKucha Night provides an encouraging, safe, community-driven event. It's a great place to break the ice and get in front of a friendly crowd with your slides.

IGNITE

Ignite is a geek event in over 100 cities worldwide. At these events, Ignite presenters share their personal and professional passions, using 20 slides that auto-advance every 15 seconds for a total of just five minutes. Ignite events can be casual gatherings in a classroom to large auditorium or theater events such as Ignite Boulder, which draws crowds of 1,000 or more.

Although an Ignite event is a lot of fast-paced fun, its success relies on planning and preparation. As Ignite Boulder co-organizer Ef Rodriguez (Figure 3-8) shares:

> We conduct a mandatory rehearsal a few weeks before the event, just to ensure that our speakers are on the right track. We work with them exhaustively, helping with slides if needed, tempering their anxieties with the realities of the event. You'll hear me say, "It's only five minutes!" a lot. It's very easy to lose sight of how little time you have on stage. Five minutes goes by in a blur. So I try to impress that upon each speaker—it's only five minutes.

FIGURE 3-8
Ef Rodriguez adds a little music to Ignite Boulder (photo by Brad Crooks).

The beauty of participating in a lightning-round event such as these is that it drives home the importance of rehearsing, and it quickly identifies nonessential content that your presentation can live without.

There are numerous presentation opportunities where time and audience attention span is short, such as an investment pitch or sales demo. Getting comfortable with 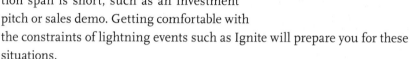 the constraints of lightning events such as Ignite will prepare you for these situations.

[**REAL-WORLD EXAMPLE**] Nikos Sarilakis of Sustainable Life Media

Sustainable Life Media (SLM) is an integrated media company that focuses on bringing about a shift toward a sustainable economy. To that end, the company promotes brands that are leading the way to this sustainable future. The company produces events, delivers information, and cultivates communities to create this flourishing future. We talked with SLM's director of marketing, Nikos Sarilakis, to learn about how SLM is using SlideShare to promote its events.

"At SLM, slideshows and videos are among the most valuable content we create," Nikos says. "We want to store them, publish them, share them, and then embed them in our website as broadly as possible."

To accomplish those goals, SLM posts many different types of content on SlideShare, including videos from its conferences, slidedecks from its speakers' presentations, press releases, brochures, and many other digital media. "SlideShare is one of the best tools to promote our conference, increase our brand awareness, and have digital content that gets a viral push in social media," Nikos says.

In addition to its public outreach efforts, SLM makes some of its videos or slideshows private and embeds them in restricted-access pages in the SLM website. The purpose of restricting access to some of its content is to allow SLM to sell it through the SLM site.

SLM's strategy with its SlideShare channel, therefore, is similar to food companies that give away free samples at the grocery store to introduce new customers to their products. As Nikos explains, "What we do and what we think works best is to upload as much valuable content as we can; tag it correctly; keep a consistent design, branding, and messaging; and share it in the right channels with the best tools. If the content is interesting, it will have results!" ◆

TED and TEDx

TED began in 1984 as a conference bringing together people from technology, entertainment, and design. The two annual TED conferences, in Long Beach/Palm Springs and Edinburgh, Scotland, feature the world's most fascinating thinkers and doers. Speakers have 18 minutes to present, a tremendous challenge since many TED speakers are used to public speaking formats where they're given an hour or more. In addition to the time constraint is the challenge of speaking about a topic they are passionate about, and which is often the focus of their life's work. The constraints of speaking at a TED conference have resulted in thought-provoking and inspiring presentations that continue to attract the world's attention.

Created in the spirit of TED's mission—"ideas worth spreading"—TEDx was "designed to give communities, organizations, and individuals the opportunity to stimulate dialogue through TED-like experiences at the local level."

TEDx events are actually licensed events with strict branding and program requirements. TEDx keeps the original TED constraints: talks are limited to 18 minutes, panels are not allowed, and the topic must not promote any commercial, religious, or political bias. Slidedecks and videos are allowed as long as the length of the presentation does not exceed 18 minutes.

TEDx speakers are not paid to present, but the cachet of presenting at the event is valuable for any public speaker wishing to expand his audience and add another feather to his public speaking cap.

The Investor Pitch Event

With the recent proliferation of startup companies, and the number of companies looking for investor funding, a new type of event has emerged: the "Pitch" event, also known as an "Investor Showcase" or "Startup Demo" event. These events are popping up in cities around the world.

Early-stage investors, known as *angel investors*, often fund young companies right on the spot, so the stakes are high for startups to create informative and engaging pitch presentations. The pitch is typically less than 10 minutes, with a 5-minute prepared presentation and 5-minute Q&A. The questions may come from the audience, or specifically from a panel of investors, as shown in Figure 3-9.

FIGURE 3-9
Investors give
immediate
feedback to an
entrepreneur
during a Women
2.0 pitch event
(photo by Michael
O'Donnell).

FIGURE 3-9 Investors give immediate feedback to an entrepreneur during a Women 2.0 pitch event (photo by Michael O'Donnell).

The audience attending the pitch event may be invitation-only, limited to qualified investors, and/or have paid a fee to attend. Some pitch events are held at the end of a startup incubator program, where the graduating founders are given an opportunity to pitch their companies to the incubator's network of investors.

Pitch events also occur on a regular basis as local meetups or as a value-added supplement to a larger event. If you're presenting at a pitch event, pay careful attention to details when creating your pitch-event presentation. The visual slidedeck must fit your presentation like a glove.

If your startup company has created a product demo, it may be tempting to present the demo during the pitch. But keep in mind, this introduces several risks, plus it consumes valuable time that might be better used describing all of the important market and business model information that investors will want to know about the company as a whole. A pitch is never just about the product or service offered; investors are looking at the entire company and plan as a package, before they write that highly coveted first check.

Even more than Ignite events, pitch events require practice. Alex White, CEO of Next Big Sound, describes his experience in Brad Feld's and David Cohen's book *Do More Faster* (Wiley):

I practiced like crazy. I must have rewritten our pitch 100 times and practiced it 500 times. The benefit of running it past dozens of people for feedback was invaluable because it's nearly impossible to separate yourself from the day-to-day business long enough to put together a high-level pitch that makes any sense. By the time we got to TechStars Demo Day, I had well-rehearsed answers to every question I was asked.

Given the high stakes involved in pitch events, practicing your talk and streamlining it with your slides is the key to your success that day.

Summary Tips

Speakers:

▶ Get started building your confidence by speaking to small groups, and include a short slidedeck.

▶ Prepare for the event by researching the audience and making sure you bring along backup technology.

▶ Spend time with the audience and participate in the rest of the event.

▶ Remember that event scouts may be in the audience, and are evaluating you for future speaking gigs.

Organizers:

▶ Use event hashtags to let users find all the presentations related to your event.

▶ Create a SlideShare account specifically for the event.

▶ Upload a promotional slidedeck to SlideShare before the event to publicize it and help attendees choose among sessions.

▶ Encourage speakers to upload slides to your event account, as well as to their own SlideShare accounts, for increased visibility.

▶ Tag presentations with keywords about the event, topic, and speaker.

▶ Use SlideShare during the event to let users view and share content in real time during the presentation.

▶ Create a SlideShare PRO or Custom channel to capture leads on who is viewing the information and how they are interacting with presentations.

Content Marketing

Marketing through valuable content (known as *content marketing*) rather than just ad messages establishes trust, credibility, and authority. For example, through content marketing you can tell a story—of your company, your brand, or you personally—that builds trust because your audience gets to understand your background. Content marketing also lets you provide valuable information, not just a jingle, to your customers and potential customers, which positions you as an expert and a trusted resource. Slidedecks showcase your expertise, especially in business-to-business (B2B) relationships.

More than 90% of B2B purchases start with content engagement, according to research by DemandGen. In fact, DemandGen reported that more than 40% of B2B buyers had their first contact with a solution provider after downloading their content. So, buyers start with content to help them make a purchasing decision. You need to be on their radar. What's more, your competitors are doing it. Indeed, 65% of companies surveyed said they would likely increase spending on content next year.

Identifying Sources of Content

But what *type* of content should you create? You have plenty of options, and SlideShare supports not only presentations but also documents, PDF, video, and audio. In addition to slidedecks, you can also upload case studies, white papers, and brochures. The audio and video aspects of SlideShare mean that you can make a webinar, synchronize your audio to your slides, and then use Leadshare to capture leads before, during, and after the webinar.

> [**TIP**] **Engage with Empathy**
>
> When thinking about the right type of content to create or share, picture your customers. What key business problems do they face? If that feels too open-ended as a starting point, look at it from a time standpoint. What short-term, medium-term, or long-term issues do they face? Then create slides to match those problems with solutions. If your company can provide those solutions, that's great. If not, don't let that stop you from writing about those solutions anyway. You'll demonstrate your expertise and your willingness to put your customers first. Your readiness to help them solve their problems—even if the solution doesn't directly involve you—shows your commitment to them.

Chances are, your organization has already created all sorts of content for you to access and share. Sales reps' presentations are the fastest win. Author and former editor-in-chief and executive editor of *Computerworld* Paul Gillin, for example, reports getting 10,000 views on slidedecks he's created for other purposes anyway. But you can also look further: have any executives given speeches? If those speeches have been recorded in audio or video, you can embed that in a presentation. Looking further still, talk with other employees in your organization, such as engineers or scientists. Ask if any of them have participated in an industry conference. If so, you can put up those presentations.

If you have a Frequently Asked Questions (FAQ) section on your website, these topics could be the basis of blog posts or short articles. And go to your training or Human Resources department and ask if they have created any instructional videos. Instructional videos are a great source of SlideShare content. Even your accounting department might be a source of content: have they built spreadsheet templates that could be useful to others? This type of content lies hidden in companies, but it could provide useful fodder for your content marketing efforts.

Your Presentation Content Strategy

When it comes to publishing presentations, three elements of content marketing offer powerful reasons to include presentations in your strategy: storytelling, search engine optimization (SEO), and content curation. Storytelling is a way to convey your message in a memorable way. Understanding how to leverage SEO will help users find your content. Curation by editors and publishers will put your content in the line of sight of the very viewers you hope to reach.

It's worth looking at how these three components of content marketing fit together. First, to have your presentation reach the greatest number of people, you want users to be able to find and share your presentation. SlideShare is integrated with the largest social sharing platforms. With one click, viewers can use the buttons in the share bar on the left side of the player to share your presentation with their social networks, as shown in Figure 4-1.

From here it can be scoop'd, storified, pinned, liked, and shared again.

FIGURE 4-1
Create content once and share it multiple times.

Storytelling in Presentations

Why are we talking about storytelling in a book about visual communication? Storytelling is one element that many presenters overlook, but it's critical to making presentations as memorable as they can possibly be. Without a story to tie your key points together, your presentation isn't much more than a series of slides with images and text. No matter how experienced a presenter you are, or how beautifully designed your slides are, the *story* is what will make your presentation memorable.

The stories we share strengthen our connectedness. Presentations created in story form have a greater possibility of connecting with the audience. A story is human. It can convey a shared experience and inspire hope in an audience that is uncertain or struggling with a new situation or unpredictable outcome. For example, in the tumultuous world of new startup businesses, the most encouraging and inspiring stories are not about the founder's achievements. Instead, the most uplifting stories often describe how a company hit its lowest point and how the founder is still standing. This is what inspires risk takers and first adopters to keep going.

A story says, "no matter what, you can do this." A story provides context, perhaps using myth or metaphor, to show viewers how to overcome similar obstacles they might be experiencing.

[REAL-WORLD EXAMPLE] # Jeremiah Owyang of Altimeter Group

 Jeremiah Owyang is a founding partner and researcher at Altimeter Group, a Silicon Valley research and analysis firm founded by Charlene Li, specializing in the technologies and trends that are disrupting businesses. Altimeter's research reports consistently rank in the top 100 most-viewed documents on SlideShare.

Altimeter Group has a clearly defined business model about what to do with the research it conducts.

This model includes summarizing the research findings in presentations, uploading them to SlideShare, and making them available for anyone to see. Across the research industry, a typical research analyst report costs between $30,000 and $80,000, averaging around $50,000. But Altimeter publishes its reports at no cost. "So the business model has to support revenue, and we're a healthy company," says Jeremiah. Altimeter follows an "open" model of publishing/

licensing, but it keeps its *research methodology* closed, as other analyst firms do.

Altimeter employs the same "converged media strategy" that it recommends to its clients, as illustrated in Figure 4-2.

Jeremiah describes how the Altimeter Group's analyst, marketing, and design teams assemble a presentation and use SlideShare as a primary vehicle for publishing their research results:

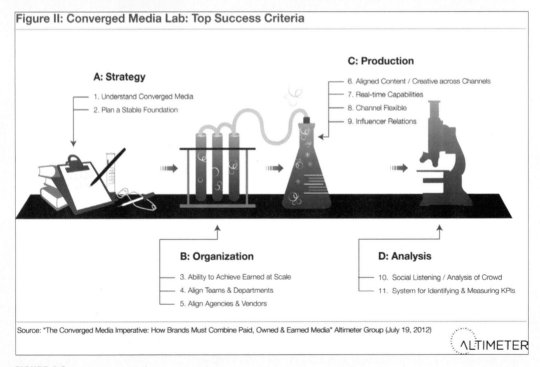

Figure II: Converged Media Lab: Top Success Criteria

A: Strategy
1. Understand Converged Media
2. Plan a Stable Foundation

C: Production
6. Aligned Content / Creative across Channels
7. Real-time Capabilities
8. Channel Flexible
9. Influencer Relations

B: Organization
3. Ability to Achieve Earned at Scale
4. Align Teams & Departments
5. Align Agencies & Vendors

D: Analysis
10. Social Listening / Analysis of Crowd
11. System for Identifying & Measuring KPIs

Source: "The Converged Media Imperative: How Brands Must Combine Paid, Owned & Earned Media" Altimeter Group (July 19, 2012)

ΛLTIMETER

FIGURE 4-2
Altimeter Group has defined success criteria for a converged media strategy.

- ▶ The content editor summarizes the results into concentrated, slide-sized content chunks.
- ▶ Altimeter's graphic design firm creates original images (no stock imagery is used).
- ▶ Designers follow the company style guide in order to maintain visual consistency for the Altimeter brand.
- ▶ A designer inserts the illustrated content into Altimeter's presentation template, creating the finished report.
- ▶ The editor then uploads the presentation to SlideShare and sets it to "private."
- ▶ The editor then uploads images from Flickr for further distribution.
- ▶ The marketing team sends the presentation as an *embargo preview* to a select group of influencers and press 48–72 hours before publication.
- ▶ The primary researchers write a blog post, describing the research project and its results.

- ▶ The marketing team makes the presentation public on SlideShare, and publishes the blog post with the embedded slideshow.

Jeremiah and the team set aside time to watch the online reactions and social sharing of each report they publish on SlideShare. "We have a funnel that measures the success of our research," Jeremiah says. "At the top of the funnel is viewer count. Then we start tracking engagement rates and reviews." The team at Altimeter is very interested in who downloads their presentations. High download numbers indicate deeper interest and connection with the report. The team enters all leads generated from the report into the company's customer relationship management database.

When a viewer embeds the report on his or her blog, Jeremiah links back to that blog in every case, whether the blog post was positive or negative (as long as it was thoughtful). He blocks out time to respond to questions, comments, and inquiries. The rest of the team embeds the report wherever they can. Why make time for engaging with viewers of the report? Jeremiah says that taking an open approach to publishing their research reports is an investment. Publishing reports on SlideShare shortens the sales cycle, because potential customers have already read Altimeter reports, so they are familiar with Altimeter's areas of expertise and quality.

Why does Altimeter follow a model of open research? "This is how we compete with larger, established firms," Jeremiah explains. "When buyers are looking for information, they're going to find us first. People regularly tell us that they use our content in their presentations to content marketing officers all the time."

This model of open research has served the firm well, establishing its credibility and reputation as a trusted resource of business intelligence for the professional world. ◆

[REAL-WORLD EXAMPLE] Samantha Starmer of REI

With so much information bombarding conference attendees during an event, it's easy to overwhelm and saturate an audience with facts, figures, and data. A skilled storyteller can form a deeper connection with each audience member by sharing knowledge in story form.

Samantha Starmer (*http://www.slideshare.net/sstarmer*) leads cross-channel experience, design, and information architecture teams at REI (*http://www.rei.com/*). An active public speaker, Samantha has evolved her presentation style to include storytelling. Audience members quickly forget that they're in a conference room or auditorium, and they are immediately drawn in as Samantha's story unfolds.

Samantha speaks frequently at professional conferences, on both retail-specific topics and best practices for user experience. She changed her presentation style based on her own experience as a conference attendee. She kept finding that as an audience member, she just wanted to get up and leave—even when there was value in what the presenter was saying—if she didn't hear an engaging story.

The value of an engaging story hit home for Samantha when she brought on Jonathon Colman to manage SEO for REI. Jonathon gave a presentation to the team about what SEO is, and he did it by telling a story. Samantha saw how well it resonated with the audience, which inspired her to reexamine how her own presentations might better connect with her listeners.

Samantha gave a presentation for the Intelligent Content conference a few years ago on user experience design. The days leading up to the conference were busy for her, and she hadn't put the structure into the presentation yet. When she arrived at the conference venue in Palm Springs, she took a walk around the grounds and noticed something about the hotel: it had a policy of no signs. This had an impact on how she felt about the hotel and whether she would come back in the future. As she walked and became more frustrated with the lack of signs to give direction, Samantha saw the connection between designing navigation and the customer experience.

She recognized that she could convey this message by telling the story of her own frustrating experience. Samantha carries her camera with her when she travels, so she quickly snapped some photos of the unsigned hotel grounds. Once she put the photos in a sequence, the story about signs (or the lack of signs) came together, as shown in Figure 4-3.

Right off the bat as Samantha started her story, she saw people nodding and laughing, frowning, emotionally reacting in a different way. Clearly, other attendees of the conference had shared the same experience. Now, she begins her presentations with that story because it creates a different kind of relationship with the audience. Samantha can tell that it connects people right away.

Samantha says that now she is consciously looking for stories, constantly pulling out her iPhone and taking photos, not really knowing what the photos will turn into. She lets the photos percolate a bit and then the story unfolds. Here's how Samantha describes the process:

> Be always ready and open to absorb a story and portions of a story. I'm always attuned now to situations that might help me tell a story—or images or comments. Have your high-level theme in your mind first; then make sure that it ties to the story you're trying to tell. The pictures that I take are less around the photos themselves and more around telling a story, all the time keeping in mind the point you're trying to make. I personally wouldn't go out seeking a story. It just never works; it

needs to happen to me instead. It's a part of my consciousness all the time.

To use Samantha's process for putting a presentation together in story form, follow these four steps:

1. Start with the outline of the point you're trying to make. This can be just a couple of text-only slides.

2. Layer the pictures on top of your outline. You'll probably end up with way more than you need to use.

3. Eliminate images until the presentation is the right length.

4. While rehearsing your talk, continue to winnow slides back to those that most strongly reinforce the main point you want your story to make.

Sometimes, crafting the story can take on a life of its own and hijack your talk. Don't let that happen to you. Make sure the story reinforces the main point of your talk. The story should serve your purpose, not confuse it with too many extraneous details. Samantha shares this advice:

It's easy to get so wrapped up in the story that it's not relevant to the point you're trying to make in the presentation. I always have to remember the point of the presentation; it's easy to go too far with the story or get into details that don't have anything to do with the point. You have to keep it honed back in to the presentation. I'm always looking for story opportunities, but I'm always conscious of the point of the story.

A compelling story puts people in the context of what you're trying to convey. This is especially true in a conference situation. The audience can more quickly understand the point of what you're trying to say, because they personally identify with the context you've set in the story. ◆

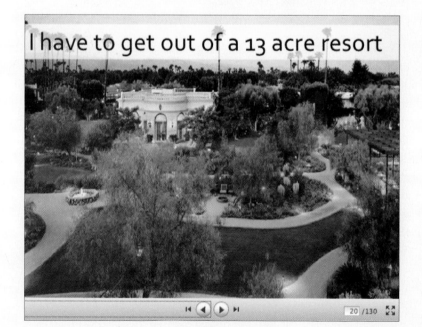

FIGURE 4-3
Photos of Samantha's experience add to her storytelling.

Next time you're at a public speaking event, a conference, or local meetup, count how many stories the keynote speaker tells. And how many stories within a story. You'll see that the best speakers are great storytellers.

Search Engine Optimization

One reason professionals visit SlideShare so often is because SlideShare presentations index quickly and highly in Google. Bill Elward of Castle Ink considers SlideShare to be an important part of his search engine optimization efforts (*http://bit.ly/pOM5If*). "Google loves to index SlideShare content," he says, "so build a small presentation about your business that includes a live link to your site. Chances are excellent that Google will crawl and index your SlideShare presentation."

SlideShare is known for its quality, which brings viewers back and entices them to spend time on the site (the average visitor views 20 slides per visit). As SlideShare's Ross Mayfield notes in the first point in his "*7 Secrets to Becoming a SlideShare Power User*" blog post (*http://bit.ly/WULiKO*):

> ***Most of your viewers come from search.*** *Presentations are just the kind of thing search engines love to eat. When creating a presentation, you tend to pick your words carefully, and that text is somewhere between the terseness of a tweet and the verbosity of a blog post. When you upload content, pay particular attention to the keywords you use in your title, description, and tags (in that order) to make your content more findable. Also, note that SlideShare extracts the text from your file and presents it as a transcript below your slides. This transcript is read by search engines, so your actual content matters.*

As more and more content and viewers come online, the importance of optimizing your content increases. Google uses approximately 200 attributes in different combinations as it scours the Web for the most relevant search results. And Bing's popularity is growing.

Google is increasingly using a content author's social sharing data to determine where your content ranks in search results. Facebook EdgeRank, Google's AuthorRank, and websites designed for viewing on mobile devices are all trying to outdo each other to deliver strong results. To give your presentations the best chances of discovery, you'll want to take advantage of SlideShare's inherent search-friendly features and its social sharing.

SHARE FOR OPTIMIZATION

Rand Fishkin is the founder and CEO of SEOMoz, a search optimization and social monitoring software company in Seattle, Washington. Rand and the SEOMoz team are active users of SlideShare, both individually and for their event, MOZCon. Rand shares how he uses SlideShare and why it is an essential part of SEOMoz's inbound marketing strategy: "SlideShare is an automatic way to share more than just on my own website. It has its own network. I include it with Twitter, Facebook, and Google+ in my thinking."

Rand likes that SlideShare is an easy medium to post to, and that it has high domain authority. The SEOMoz team has found that by using the right keywords, their presentations rank high in search results. Embedding a presentation in a blog post helps it rank even higher.

> **[TIP] Use the Google Keywords Tool**
>
> Rand recommends using the keywords tool on Google to identify keywords to include in your presentation title and text. Click Exact Match to see the results. Don't add everything—just the keywords that are relative to your presentation.

DEVELOP INBOUND LINKS

You can also increase traffic to your presentations by getting traffic from other sites. Rand has found that it is valuable to promote his SlideShare presentations externally, from other locations. Having other websites embed his presentations is one of the most valuable ways to generate traffic. Not only does the view count increase, but the presentations are also reaching the bloggers' audience, increasing the overall reach of the SEOMoz brand.

Rand also recommends including links within your slidedeck:

I know I'm making friends with everyone who is linked in my slideshow. They express thanks on Twitter and often reciprocate. In addition, there are 20% to 30% who will point back to articles I've written or tools on my site, sending traffic back to where it can convert to sales.

This is particularly important to SEOMoz, which relies on inbound marketing for all of its sales.

Rand makes the most out of SlideShare's network when he presents to a live audience. Before he goes onstage, he tweets the link to his SlideShare deck and includes the URL of the deck in the presentation itself (as shown in Figure 4-4), which increases sharing activity.

Because SlideShare automatically transcribes the text in your presentation when you upload, it is easy for search engines to find you. If you have given a live presentation, and your slidedeck contains mostly images and not enough text to give it context, add your own text transcription to help with your SEO.

POSITION YOURSELF WITH AUTHORRANK

As the Web becomes more social, savvy content marketers are also paying attention to the way Google ranks content based on social sharing. By paying attention to these "social signals," Google has added a way to use your own social network to help it rank your content.

To ensure your content benefits from Google's sharing measurement, make your share buttons easy to find. Share your presentations on all your social platforms, and encourage viewers to share as well. Reach out to influencers and ask them to share your presentation, and be sure to reciprocate.

Recently, Google introduced a new metric that has quickly gotten SEO experts' attention: AuthorRank. This new piece of the SEO puzzle measures the authority and reputation of the author. In other words, Google is looking not only at your content, but also at *you*. Your reputation as a content creator will influence your content's ranking in search results. AuthorRank directly associates content to the author's Google+ profile, and it displays a rich snippet of that profile (the author's photo) in search results. Understanding your role as an author of content will give you the edge in rankings when your presentations are competing for attention.

Content Curation

Even the most compelling presentations in the world are competing with all of the other content available on the Web. Now that we've explored the importance of storytelling in presentations, and how to use search engine optimization to your advantage, it's time to look at a couple of the most powerful curation platforms and how your presentations can get more views and traffic from these communities.

You become a content *curator* when you invoke your own expertise and experience into selecting existing content, and then publish it in a single location with your own comments. Curation is a great way to become familiar with the subject matter or platform that you're curating. The criteria for selection might evolve organically as you see what your readers or viewers respond to. Or it may be based on defined business goals, with a particular purpose in mind.

Anytime you see an article or blog post titled, say, "5 favorite (content items)," that is an example of curated content.

[TIP]   How to Create a Quick Blog Post

Need a quick blog post? Search SlideShare for presentations on a particular topic. Embed the slideshows in your blog post. Write a few lines of commentary to give context for each slideshow. The slideshows bring variety, perspective, and background to a blog post without your having to do all the research yourself. Leveraging others' slidedecks with proper credit will bring you additional benefits of retweets and sharing, because the SlideShare authors will likely be sharing your blog post further, just as Jeremiah does when others embed Altimeter's slides in their blog posts.

It's important to remember that curation is different from *aggregation*. Aggregated content doesn't have the editorial richness that curated content provides. Aggregation just supplies the links and titles of articles, as you'll find at Alltop, Google, or Yahoo! News alerts. Curated content, on the other hand, requires subjective discretion, a human decision to select a certain piece.

USING PINTEREST WITH SLIDESHARE

Pinterest (*http://www.pinterest.com*) is a highly visual content-sharing website. It functions as both a social networking service and content curation tool that allows users to *pin* images, videos, and other web content (such as slideshows) to topical *boards* that friends or connections can follow or share (*repinning*).

In the relatively short time it's been around, Pinterest has quickly caught the attention of marketers because of its vast number of users and the prodigious volume of content that has been pinned. According to Pew Research Center's Internet & American Life Project, at the end of 2012, 15% of all Internet users worldwide use Pinterest. What's more, Pinterest drives more ecommerce orders than either Twitter or Facebook.

Large retailers such as Nordstrom and Walmart have taken notice and are investing time and resources in managing their Pinterest presence. Small businesses, startups, nonprofits, and entrepreneurs can use the same techniques and best practices as the big companies to increase the reach of their content and extend its findability. For content creators and marketers, engagement and viral sharing are the foundation of a strong content marketing strategy.

Pinterest has integrated with SlideShare to create one-click pinning of SlideShare presentations. Savvy content marketers are using SlideShare and Pinterest together to create visibility and customer engagement with content.

You might wonder why you should bother using Pinterest if your presentations are already uploaded on SlideShare. The answer lies in the viral sharing power of the Pinterest user community and the power of the repin. If you're a Twitter user, you understand the exponential sharing power of a *retweet*. The same applies to Pinterest. When your SlideShare presentation is pinned by a Pinterest user, all of her Pinterest followers will view it in their Pinterest streams. When the followers repin, your presentation is off and running!

You can pin SlideShare presentations to your Pinterest boards in two ways. First, you can click the "Pin it" button displayed in the column of social sharing buttons to the left of your SlideShare presentation, as shown in Figure 4-5.

Or, if you do a lot of pinning around the Web and want an easy way to pin any kind of content quickly, you can add the *"Pin it" bookmarklet (http://about.pinterest.com/goodies)* to your browser's toolbar, as shown in Figure 4-6. Clicking the bookmarklet from any site will allow you to pin that page's content to a board on Pinterest.

FIGURE 4-5
Use the "Pin it" button in the share bar to pin a presentation to a Pinterest board.

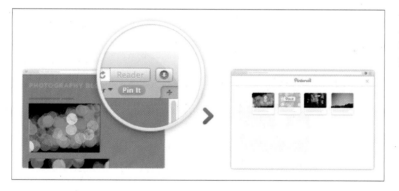

FIGURE 4-6
Add the Pinterest bookmarklet to your browser toolbar.

Either method of pinning (clicking "Pin it" next to a presentation or clicking the "Pin it" bookmarklet while on a presentation page) will open the Pin It window shown in Figure 4-7.

FIGURE 4-7
Select the board to
pin to, and edit the
description.

FIGURE 4-7
Select the board to pin to, and edit the description.

Just select which of your Pinterest boards you want to pin the presentation to, add or edit the text description as you like, and click on the red Pin It button.

Encourage viewers of your presentations to pin them. And be sure to make the most of your Pinterest sharing capability by pinning your own presentations to one of your Pinterest boards.

Find things to pin

SlideShare is a great place to engage with the Pinterest community around presentations and public speaking. If you're not sure where to find things to pin, add */source/* with a domain name to the Pinterest URL to see what has been pinned from a specific website, like this:

http://pinterest.com/source/<domainname>.com

For example, to see the latest pins from Haiku Deck, type the URL *http://pinterest.com/source/haikudeck.com* in your browser. Items that people have pinned will display under "Pins from Haikudeck.com," as shown in Figure 4-8.

By using this *source/<domainname>.com* technique, you can see what users have pinned and what has been the most popular. This can help you strategize what types of items you might want to pin yourself.

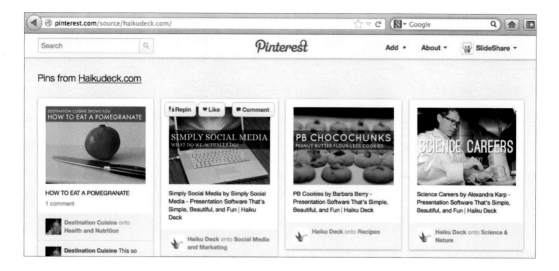

Build your Pinterest community

Pinterest is an effective way of getting the attention of influencers. As with other social publishing platforms, tagging and commenting on their pins will get you on their radar.

As you search Pinterest, you can:

- Discover what items people are pinning from your or another specific website.
- Get inspiration for creating a new presentation.
- Engage with the Pinterest community by pinning content.
- Increase views of your presentations by encouraging viewers to pin and repin.

When viewers pin your presentation, they are also offered the opportunity to post on Twitter and Facebook, for even more sharing!

Eight ways to increase your Pinfluence

With the recent integration of Pinterest tools into the SlideShare platform, it's even easier to use the two social media platforms collaboratively to get your message out to the world. Pinterest marketing expert Beth Hayden, author of *Pinfluence: The Complete Guide to Marketing Your Business with Pinterest* (Wiley), shares eight ideas for using Pinterest and SlideShare together:

FIGURE 4-8
Use /source/
<domainname>.com
to find what has been
pinned from a specific
website.

1. Practice content curation.

   One of the most effective ways to use Pinterest is to establish yourself as a trusted expert in your field, and the best way to do this is by becoming a content curator on your topic. Handpick the best blog posts, web pages, images, and presentations, and pin them to your Pinterest boards. Pin presentations to your existing boards or create new pinboards highlighting SlideShare decks exclusively.

2. Book more speaking engagements by pinning sample presentations.

   Try creating a Pinterest board dedicated to your best SlideShare decks. You can even take this idea one step further, as educator and marketer Mark Johnson has. As shown in Figure 4-9, he created an entire Pinterest résumé with pins of his best presentations.

FIGURE 4-9
Create an entire Pinterest résumé with links to your best presentations on SlideShare.

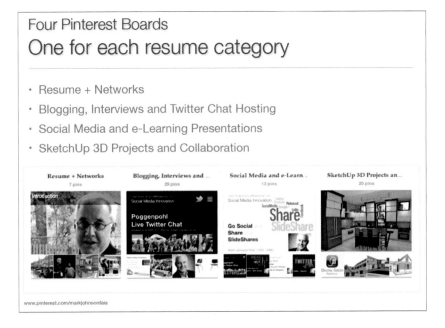

3. Use Pinterest to distribute and publicize your SlideShare presentations.

   Pinterest currently drives more referral traffic to websites and blogs than Twitter, Linkedin, or YouTube. Why not leverage that referral traffic potential to drive visitors to your SlideShare channel? All you need to do is pin your newest presentations to your Pinterest boards, just as you would tweet them or share them on Facebook or LinkedIn.

4. Use SlideShare to distribute and publicize your Pinterest content.

   Create a SlideShare presentation about how you're using Pinterest and how it's working for you. People are hankering for new and interesting ways to use Pinterest for marketing their messages. If you create an instructional presentation that includes new Pinterest techniques (and include a link to your Pinterest profile URL at the end), you're bound to pick up some new followers. You'll get views for your SlideShare presentation *and* build your Pinterest platform at the same time.

5. Drive people to your mailing list offers.

   When you're giving away a free report, video, or other freebie on your website or blog, make sure to add that offer to the last page of your SlideShare presentation. If it's done in a compelling way using good copywriting techniques, your Pinterest followers will want to go to your website and sign up for your list. This is a great way of building your email list without being overly sales-y or pushy.

6. Create collaborative boards for conferences.

   When you're speaking at conferences and events, pin your SlideShare presentations from the events. You can invite other presenters and speakers to pin their presentations from the conference too. Ask them to be collaborators on your Pinterest boards, so they can upload their photos and resources.

7. Use Pinterest to help you find your presentation voice and personality.

   Pinterest can be a source of inspiration to help you develop your personal speaking style. Use Pinterest to collect ideas, quotes, images, and presentations that inspire you. Then revisit those inspirational boards when you're ready to write your presentation and create your slides. Perusing Pinterest can spark your imagination, especially if you're feeling stuck about what to do next.

8. Create a dedicated board that tells the story of your business.

   Describe how your company was founded and what your values are. Create a SlideShare presentation that includes your staff's photos and bios or behind-the-scenes photos, and pin them to your company storyboard. Make sure to include customer success stories too.

It's important to remember that Pinterest content has a short shelf life. In other words, its pins are shooting stars compared to SlideShare presentations, which are more like comets. So make sure to stay active with both your pinning and your content.

USING SCOOP.IT WITH SLIDESHARE

Recognizing the importance of content curation, SlideShare also integrates with *Scoop.it (http://www.scoop.it)*, a software tool and curation publishing platform, to make it easier for SlideShare users to share presentations in a digital custom-newspaper format. Scoop.it lets you create online magazines of content that you curate based on your interests and expertise.

For example, you can find slidedecks related to K–12 education and publish a weekly Scoop.it magazine that shares those decks more widely. It's much more likely that you will curate content on a regular basis if you use software tools like Scoop.it, because doing so makes the process quick and easy. Make it part of your daily or weekly routine to select and share a presentation.

Slide presentations are particularly popular with Scoop.it curators because they're visual, interactive, engaging, and embeddable. Presentation designers want their presentations curated because curators endorse great content, bring context, spread and share, and have qualified audiences on specific topics.

You can publish SlideShare presentations as embedded presentations on your Scoop.it topic page and share them with all your social media channels. If you already curate content for an online magazine, you can now include SlideShare presentations with just a few clicks.

Here's how to get started curating content with Scoop.it:

1. Create your account.

   Be careful when you choose your username, because it will constitute your profile URL on which your topics will be listed.

2. Create a topic and install the bookmarklet.

   Once you've confirmed your email, create your first topic and install the bookmarklet. Or just skip this step by clicking Next and follow the "Skip this step for now" link.

   To create a topic, mouse over the My Topics tab in the top bar and click "Create a Topic" to bring up the dialog box shown in Figure 4-10.

FIGURE 4-10
Create a topic in
Scoop.it and start
curating.

3. Follow other topics.

The last step is to follow other topics to start your Community. Enter keywords in the search bar to find topics you might be interested in. Follow those you want by clicking the blue Follow button available for each topic. When you're finished building your Community, click Complete to access your dashboard.

There are four ways to curate content on a topic using Scoop.it:

Rescoop content from your followed topics

When you find a relevant presentation on one of the topics you follow that you'd also like to publish on yours, just click on the Rescoop button located at the top right of each article.

Accept a post suggested by the suggestion engine

At the top of your Scoop.it page, mouse over the My Topics tab and select the topic about which you want to publish content to be redirected to its Curate page.

Create a post

Use the New Post button located at the top of your Scoop.it page. Paste a URL in the dedicated field and click on the blue button with the two white arrows. The system will then automatically extract the title, picture/video/PDF, and description, which you can edit as you wish.

Grab content while navigating the Web

Find something you'd like to capture and share, and then click the Scoop.it bookmarklet that you've added to your toolbar.

Other Scoop.it users, as well as visitors of your topics, can suggest content to your topics (by using the Suggest button in your topic tool bar, which replaces the New Post button for visitors) or by using the bookmarklet themselves. Content suggested by users will appear in your list of suggested content, in addition to content suggested by the Scoop.it recommendation engine. You can decide to accept any item by clicking on the appropriate Scoop.it button.

You can also source relevant presentations for your Scoop.it topics. Create a topic in Scoop.it, and then curate and add items to that topic. If you're already a Scoop.it user, click on your toolbar widget to scoop a presentation, right from the SlideShare page.

Take advantage of the customization feature called Insight, which allows you to quickly personalize any article, image, or video by adding commentary. Scoop.it has also added more robust social integration, allowing users to sign in via LinkedIn and to view their social connections on Twitter, Facebook, and LinkedIn to see which topics they're currently creating. Scoop.it's notification functionality encourages social-graph-based discovery.

Once you're comfortable using Scoop.it, try scooping a presentation and then pinning it to your Pinterest board. All three tools work together: publish on SlideShare, curate with Scoop.it, and share with Pinterest. Visit the Scoop.it website to find out more about advanced options for sharing and embedding Scoop.it topics.

Summary Tips

▶ More than 90% of B2B purchases start with content engagement, so use slide decks to showcase your expertise. SlideShare presentations index quickly and highly in Google due to SlideShare's high domain authority.

▶ SlideShare lets you upload other content formats besides slides, such as PDF documents, audio and video, which means you can upload a speech or webinar as well.

▶ Use the keywords tool on Google to identify keywords to include in your presentation title and text.

▶ Tell the story of your company, your brand, or of you personally to build trust with your audience.

▶ If you're short on time, look for content you've already created that you can re-use, such as instructional videos. Even the FAQ section of your website can spark ideas for information to share.

▶ Become a respected content curator by selecting content created by others and then publish it in a single location with your own comments.

▶ Use tools like Scoop.it to make it easier for SlideShare users to share curated presentations.

▶ Pin SlideShare presentations to your Pinterest board for added exposure.

Sell, Sell, Sell

SALESPEOPLE TODAY FACE A tougher environment than in the past. First, today's buyers are short on time. Prospects no longer have the time in their schedules to go out for long, expensed lunches with salespeople. Even in industries like pharmaceutical sales, where the tradition of face-to-face sales meetings is deeply rooted, the staff of doctors' offices can't always sit down for a full hour of lunch 'n' learn as they did in the past. Often, a salesperson has only a few minutes of face time with a prospect.

Second, today's buyers are more informed. Salespeople used to be able to position themselves as subject matter experts, with exclusive knowledge about a product or service. But with the Internet, prospects can get access to product information on their own, removing the mystique and value of personal connection that the salesperson used to control and provide.

If the need for information is not there, and the time to interact in person is limited, salespeople need new ways to differentiate themselves from their competitors. Salespeople must now be problem solvers, and they must be keenly aware of trends and the future issues that their customers may face. The ability to anticipate business problems, identify the potential effect, and offer tailored solutions has created the sales methodology called *insight selling*. For today's salespeople, it's not enough to be knowledgeable about their own product features; they must be knowledgeable about their customers' businesses, including challenges and industry threats.

This is where knowledge-rich content works for sales as well as marketing. Customer stories can be created as case-study presentations that sales professionals can share with the potential customer to show their knowledge and experience in solving the customer's problem and to demonstrate success in solving similar problems for other existing customers. Ebooks and white papers can also be summarized and shared as presentations, not to mention the value of a slidedeck that captures and shows the prospect's competitive information.

According to a recent report on social selling published by Inside View:

Industry research shows that 90% of executives never respond to cold calls or unsolicited emails, yet 84% will engage with a sales person when they are connected through a friend, colleague, customer, or industry peer.

With the rapid increase in use of social tools, decision makers can now ask the social network for recommendations and feedback on potential solutions. Successful sales professionals know this, and they make it part of their sales strategy to stay visible and involved in their industry's social networks.

For more information on how Inside View uses social selling to generate its own sales, see the "Real-World Example" sidebar on Koka Sexton.

Lead Generation

Constraints on the amount of time a salesperson can spend with a prospect increase the need for marketing to provide qualified leads. Marketing initiatives for increasing revenue must be consistent with sales goals. Marketing and sales teams must work together in a coordinated manner in order to effectively convert qualified leads into sales.

Lead generation is most effective when marketing and sales teams are aligned in their goals, are using the same metrics, and have developed smooth transitions as sales leads make their way through the sales funnel.

Including visual presentations in your marketing communications strategy supports the collaboration between sales and marketing. As a creative asset, a presentation can serve the following functions:

- Demonstrate consistent messaging and branding
- Provide a lead-generation tool
- Pass lead contact info into a customer relationship management (CRM) database
- Generate metrics for numbers of views and the prospects' interaction with the asset

When the marketing team creates and uploads a presentation to SlideShare, the sales team should be notified. This gives the salesperson context for any leads that are generated from the presentation. It also serves as a basis for conversation between the salesperson and the lead.

[REAL-WORLD EXAMPLE] Koka Sexton of Inside View

Inside View's director of social media strategy, Koka Sexton, revealed how his company uses social selling to generate sales leads.

Interestingly, Koka began using SlideShare originally for research, and when he set up his company account, he initially didn't know which direction he'd be heading with it. "I first started uploading content when we had some regional marketing events that had public presentations," Koka says, describing his first steps. "When our CEO Umberto Milletti went to SXSW he gave a talk on Social Espionage & CRM: Selling to Customer 2.0. As is often the case, he had people coming up to him asking if they could get a copy of the slides, so he asked me for help. So I shared them on SlideShare."

The results brought a quick win: "Within the first hour, the SlideShare presentation had 400 hits on it. And then I realized I should start capturing leads, so I signed up for Silver Pro and turned on lead capture."

In the next day and a half, Koka got another 70 leads, which topped out the number of leads given at the Gold plan level. "At that point, I realized I needed to upgrade to Platinum where there is no lead limit, even though I didn't know what the upper volume would be," he adds. "I also realized it was time to put some

more resources into branding the InsideView Channel and more."

Upgrading to SlideShare Platinum brought additional benefits. "Initially when we were generating leads, we weren't passing them directly to sales reps. Instead, we put them into a nurturing campaign for pre-qualification," Koka explains:

> With SlideShare Platinum, we were able to add custom fields to the lead form. This allowed the leads to be scored immediately so some that met a filtering criteria could be directly assigned to reps. Now we can track lead quality, and the quality of the leads is good, which further validates the Platinum level for us.

The number and quality of the leads Koka got from SlideShare led him to rethink this strategy for the site:

> Initially, I was thinking this was a repository for data sheets and corporate functional content. But when I realized that presentations could go viral, I put more of a focus on creating more content about the industry as a whole instead of us

as a company. This quality content is a driver for our thought leadership. Now we are specifically producing for the SlideShare audience based on what we are learning from the community, what is popular, and what gains engagement.

Koka uploads content to SlideShare regularly, and he encourages sharing the content to Twitter, Facebook, and other social sharing sites. Koka also shares this lesson learned:

> One thing we tried briefly, but that didn't work, was requiring people to fill in the lead form on all of our content. We saw the numbers decline quickly. So you should make [the lead form] optional for most people. Now, for us, data sheets and company specific collateral is gated, but general thought leadership stuff we open up.

That strategy entices followers and encourages sharing of the content broadly, bringing in more viewers. The more specialized content is gated, bringing in high-quality leads. ◆

GENERATING LEADS WITH LEADSHARE (FOR PRO ACCOUNTS)

LeadShare (PRO account upgrade required) is SlideShare's lead-generation tool that lets businesses collect customer leads through their presentations, documents, and videos. When you activate LeadShare on a presentation, viewers are given the opportunity to submit their contact information in one of two ways:

- When downloading a presentation, the viewer will be first asked to fill out a short contact form.
- When the viewer is browsing through a presentation, the contact form will appear as a pop-up form.

The pop-up form appears when someone is viewing your slides on SlideShare, as well as when your presentation is embedded in an article or blog post on another website. To take advantage of this feature and generate the most leads, encourage writers and publishers to embed your presentations in their articles. Any viewer (including those not registered as SlideShare users) can submit the LeadShare pop-up form, but only registered SlideShare users can download a presentation.

To start a LeadShare campaign, upload a file to SlideShare and then follow these steps:

1. Select PRO Dashboard from the drop-down menu at the top right of any page.
2. Select "Start a new campaign" in the Capture Leads section. On the next page, shown in Figure 5-1, you'll set up your LeadShare form, using the default language or customizing the wording as you wish.
3. Give your campaign a name in the "Campaign name" field. (This is for your personal use in your notes; it won't display on the lead form.)
4. The Title field is your call to action for the viewer. Make sure the title grabs your viewer's attention and interest.
5. Enter your message text in the Subtitle field, customizing it for your company's voice and style, as shown in the "Include a Call to Action" sidebar.
6. You'll see a preview window, where you can double-check how your text reads.
7. Gold and Platinum accounts will be given the option to select target geography. The default is "worldwide," but you can select a specific country or region.

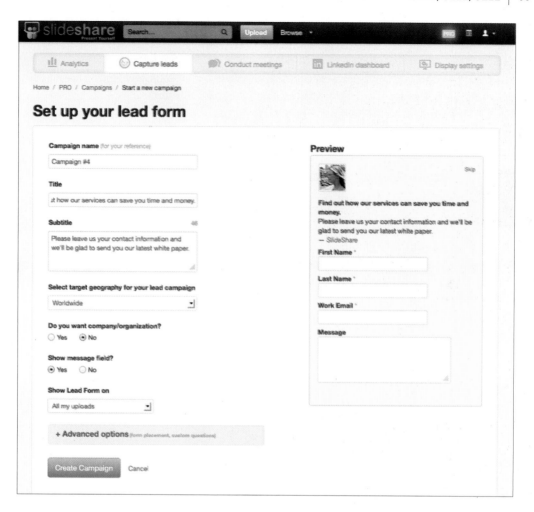

8. Select whether you'd like to require viewers to enter the name of their company or organization.

9. Select whether a text box will appear, giving viewers a chance to type in their questions or comments.

10. Select whether you'd like the LeadShare form to appear on all of your uploaded files, files with a particular tag, or only on a specific uploaded file.

Then, just click Create Campaign to launch your new LeadShare campaign.

FIGURE 5-1
The LeadShare form captures your viewers' contact information and stores it as a sales lead.

Include a Call to Action

Always include a Call to Action (CTA) in your LeadShare form. Let viewers know what they will receive in return—for example, a phone or email follow-up, addition to your newsletter, notification of upcoming events, or webinars. Figures 5-2 through 5-9 show some examples of well-written "Get in touch" buttons that work as effective CTAs. ◆

Want to know more about our products?

Please give us your contact info and we'll get back to you with details.

— Frost & Sullivan

FIGURE 5-2
This CTA is used for traditional project sales lead generation.

Like what you see? Download the summary...

...and tell us how to reach you. We will be with you shortly!

— Best Practices, LLC

FIGURE 5-3
This CTA is used for traditional lead generation.

Get More Marketing Goodness!

Want more easy-to-access Marketing Know-How? Fill out this brief form to become a free member of MarketingProfs:

— MarketingProfs

FIGURE 5-4
This "join us" CTA adds a contact database for ongoing communications.

Get Empowered with Us!

Thank you for viewing! What would really make our day is some LOVE from you! TWEET, LIKE, SHARE, and FOLLOW US on Slideshare! :)

— Empowered Presentations, Presentation Design Firm - Honolulu, HI

FIGURE 5-5
This CTA promotes community growth through social media.

Did you enjoy the read?

If you are interested in receiving updates via email, from the Talent Project Newsletter, please register below:

— *Anthony Raja Devadoss*

FIGURE 5-6
This CTA is used for newsletter signup.

Want Brand Driven Insights in Your Email Inbox?

Sign up for my newsletter to receive the latest insights on branding & digital marketing.

— *Nick Westergaard*

FIGURE 5-7
This is another CTA for newsletter signup.

Want to know more about my speaking and consulting services?

Provide your contact info and I'll get back soon with details.

— *Liz Ngonzi*

FIGURE 5-8
This CTA is used for public speaking and consulting services lead generation.

Want to talk about putting the plan in place?

Give us your contact info and we'll be in touch.

— *Barry Feldman*

FIGURE 5-9
This CTA is used for lead generation for consulting services.

LET VIEWERS GET IN TOUCH

"Get in touch" is one of the most powerful SlideShare tools to turn viewers into leads. When activated, this feature displays as a gold "Get in touch" button (as shown in Figure 5-10) at the bottom of the presentation screen.

FIGURE 5-10

The gold button enables viewers to submit their contact information while engaged with your presentation.

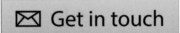

When the viewer clicks on the button, the LeadShare form displays. This convenient method of asking for a viewer's contact information is highly successful, because it occurs while the viewer is engaged with the content. Once the contact information is submitted, the button disappears and you have a new lead.

CONNECT YOUR CTA TO YOUR VALUE PROPOSITION

Jill Konrath helps sales professionals increase sales in the corporate marketplace. In her presentation "Crafting Strong Value Propositions," Jill defines a *value proposition* as "a clear statement about the outcomes that an individual or an organization can realize from using your product, service, or solution." When using a LeadShare pop-up form, your call to action should reflect (and immediately follow) the slide that contains your value proposition.

Jill goes on to say, "People only change [products or companies] if a new option is better than the status quo and can positively impact their key business drivers." Once your sales presentation demonstrates that what you're offering is worth making a change, align your LeadShare language to reflect that message.

Choose where in your presentation you'd like the LeadShare form to appear when someone is viewing the presentation, and indicate whether you'd like the form to appear when the viewer downloads the file.

If you have a Gold or Platinum account, you can require certain information, such as a mailing address or a custom question like, "How did you hear about us?" Gold account holders can ask one custom question, and Platinum account holders can include up to 10 custom questions.

While LeadShare is primarily designed as a lead collection program, the core technology is built in such a way that it can also be used for small contextual surveys. Simply set up the form and use the custom questions to ask whatever you want. You can choose from a single-line answer or multiple-choice selections in the custom questions. Once the responses are collected, you can download the data in CSV format.

A viewer will be asked to fill out your lead form only once. This eliminates duplicate work for your prospective customer and ensures you don't receive duplicate leads. As a result of this feature, your download count may be higher than your lead count.

You can *gate* the presentation, which means the viewer must complete the form in order to view the rest of the presentation. When it comes to gating a presentation, SlideShare's Kevin Fisher gives this advice:

> *If you're looking to filter for more qualified leads, make the form optional and place it at the end of the presentation. If you're going to require that the viewer fill out the LeadShare form, "gate" only 20% of the forms at most. Never gate all of them.*

There is no limit to how many campaigns you can set up, or how many documents can be part of one campaign. Choose whatever combination works for you. If you want to show the same lead collection form on all your documents, just create one campaign and put all your documents in it. If you want to show different lead forms on different documents, you can set up separate campaigns and customize your lead form for each one.

TRACK YOUR LEADS

A SlideShare PRO account provides a dashboard that allows you to track the leads generated by your LeadShare campaigns, as shown in Figure 5-11.

You can monitor lead generation for any campaign at any time. From your PRO dashboard, select View Leads. You can either click on the number below "Leads collected" to go to the leads collected page, or you can click on any of the campaign names to go to the details of the campaign. The campaign details screen will have three tabs on top:

Files Included

Lists files on which the lead form will be shown. These files can be your presentations, documents, and videos on SlideShare.

Edit Campaign

Allows you to edit or change the campaign.

Leads Collected

Lists all the leads for the campaign and the option to "Download a .CSV" file of your leads.

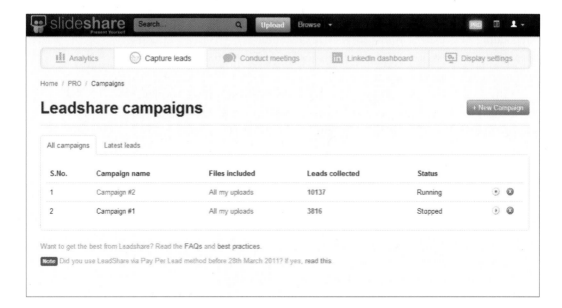

To download the CSV file that contains your leads:

1. Go to the drop-down menu on the top right of every page and select PRO Dashboard.
2. Under the Capture Leads feature, click on the Manage link.
3. Click on the download icon under the Leads Collected column. Once the CSV file has downloaded, you can view or edit it.

FEED YOUR LEADS INTO SALESFORCE

You can integrate LeadShare with Salesforce CRM, using Slide2Lead, an application developed by Mansa Systems using the LeadShare API (also by Mansa Systems). Slide2Lead provides complete synchronization of SlideShare documents, campaigns, leads, and document statistics with Salesforce, as shown in Figure 5-12.

You can either schedule synchronization or have it occur in real time. SlideShare's document statistics are imported directly into Salesforce.com.

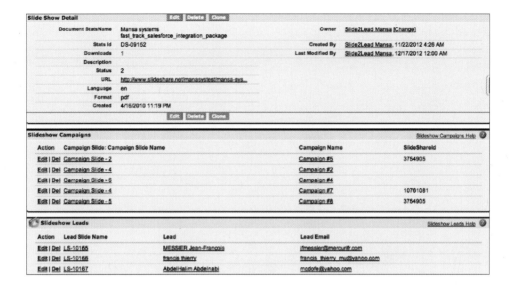

Slide Show Detail	Edit	Delete	Clone			
Document StatsName	Mansa systems fast_track_salesforce_integration_package		Owner	Slide2Lead Mansa [Change]
Stats Id	DS-09152		Created By	Slide2Lead Mansa, 11/22/2012 4:26 AM
Downloads	1		Last Modified By	Slide2Lead Mansa, 12/17/2012 12:00 AM
Description				
Status	2			
URL	http://www.slideshare.net/manasystest/mansa-sys...			
Language	en			
Format	pdf			
Created	4/16/2010 11:19 PM			

| | | | Edit | Delete | Clone |

Slideshow Campaigns — Slideshow Campaigns Help

Action	Campaign Slide: Campaign Slide Name	Campaign Name	SlideShareId
Edit | Del	Campaign Slide - 2	Campaign #5	3754905
Edit | Del	Campaign Slide - 4	Campaign #2	
Edit | Del	Campaign Slide - 6	Campaign #4	
Edit | Del	Campaign Slide - 4	Campaign #7	10761081
Edit | Del	Campaign Slide - 5	Campaign #8	3754905

Slideshow Leads — Slideshow Leads Help

Action	Lead Slide Name	Lead	Lead Email
Edit | Del	LS-10165	MESSIER Jean-François	jfmessier@mercurifr.com
Edit | Del	LS-10166	francis thierry	francis_thierry_mu@yahoo.com
Edit | Del	LS-10167	AbdelHalim Abdelnabi	mcdofe@yahoo.com

Presentations in the Entire Sales Cycle

When face-to-face time is limited, it's essential to move through a lot of information quickly. Visual presentations can support each step along the sales cycle. If the lead you have was generated by a prospect downloading a presentation, follow up by asking for the prospect's feedback on the deck. In addition, each time you upload a new presentation is an opportunity to follow up with the prospect again; it's a natural reason for a follow-up contact.

Create presentations that demonstrate a high level of understanding about the sales prospect's business. This shows your knowledge and interest in her business. Include a few images that show you've done your homework, such as an easy-to-read chart that shows the industry's latest trends, as Prophets Agency does in its "ID13, The 2013 Trends" slidedeck, shown in Figure 5-13.

FIGURE 5-12
Synchronize and manage sales leads in Salesforce with Sales2Lead.

FIGURE 5-13
Prophets Agency's
easy-to-read chart
shows that it has
done its homework
for the client.

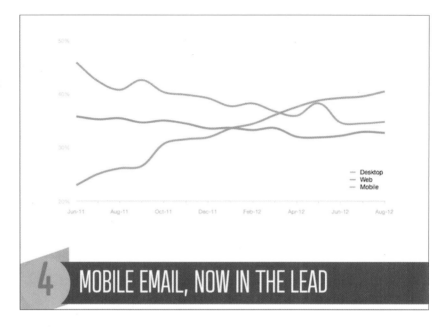

A slide with quotes from thought leaders in the space will show that you're keeping up with industry discussions. Visual snapshots are easier to remember than verbal descriptions. By sharing even a few slides, you'll demonstrate your familiarity with the industry, and your prospect will appreciate the effort you put into understanding her business and needs.

RESEARCH BEFORE MEETING WITH THE PROSPECT

Research is essential preparation for a sales meeting. To be prepared for the meeting, a successful salesperson will research not only the prospect company, but also news, financial reports, competitor information, and industry trends that paint the picture of where that prospect sits in his industry's landscape. As Stewart Brand identified in his *pace layering diagram* (see Figure 5-14), different tools have different rates of adoption and use.

Information about the prospect's competitors helps inform a tailored solution to her problems. It also helps the salesperson anticipate future threats and puts him in a consultative position with the prospect.

[**REAL-WORLD EXAMPLE**]   ## Jake Wengroff of Frost & Sullivan

Frost & Sullivan provides disciplined research and best-practice models to drive the generation, evaluation, and implementation growth strategies for its enterprise clients. The company uses SlideShare to upload presentations by its analysts. These presentations, including an archive of Analyst Briefings, serve as a resource for current and future clients.

Jake Wengroff, Global Director of Social Media at Frost & Sullivan, describes the time when the company first started to capture leads. At that time, SlideShare only offered a pay-per-lead program. The number of leads generated from Frost & Sullivan's presentations exhausted the company's budget in just two days. It was the quality of the leads, in addition to the volume, that sold Wengroff on the value of using presentations for lead generation.

As a next step, Frost & Sullivan took advantage of lead capture through a custom-branded channel. But first it needed to make a business case in order to get sign-off from the company's global president. The business case was able to tie leads to revenue, and Wengroff got the green light.

It took time to get other Frost & Sullivan groups, such as corporate communications and regional marketing people around the world, on board. Frost & Sullivan has 18 people in hybrid roles as regional directors and in corporate communications who help assemble and distribute the company's content. Not all content within the company was meant to be shared. Wengroff was able to explain what he and the team were doing with SlideShare, and how it complemented their traditional work processes.

"The biggest learning was making it relevant to our existing business systems, namely establishing a process for getting the leads into our CRM system and having a team process them," says Wengroff. "This then meant that qualifying reps needed to know about SlideShare to understand where the leads came from and how to value them. When we did this, we made SlideShare operational, and effectively aligned it with existing processes to grow revenue."

When a lead comes in from SlideShare, it's sent to Frost & Sullivan's lead processing team, which qualifies the leads. Some of the leads are simply students doing research, but stronger leads come from major companies that are interested in more information about Frost & Sullivan research.

"We have even received SlideShare leads from existing Frost & Sullivan clients who found our presentations through an online search—validating the idea that individuals often revert to regular Internet searches rather than first contacting their research provider, but also validating the strength of our presence on SlideShare and the social web," Wengroff says.

Wengroff offers these suggestions for other companies using LeadShare:

▶ Take the time to customize your LeadShare form so you are collecting the information you need.

▶ Don't get overwhelmed with the number of leads coming in.

▶ Review each lead and determine if it is significant enough for follow-up.

▶ Take the time to train the individuals who will be processing these leads so they know where they originated from and how to best continue contact.

▶ Be patient. The more you stick with the lead processing, the more likely you are to have some leads convert into new business for your company.

Frost & Sullivan's results from using LeadShare were impressive. For an investment of $299/month for its PRO Platinum account, it gained 1,300 qualified leads, which generated $125,000 in revenue. ◆

FIGURE 5-14
Stewart Brand
presents his pace
layering diagram
(photo courtesy of
Mike Lee).

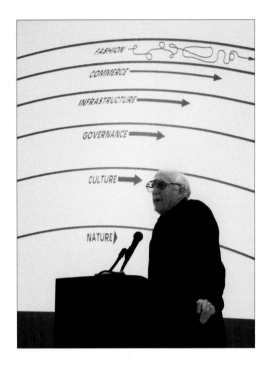

Research also helps prepare the salesperson to make sure he is solving the right problem for the customer. Stepping back and taking a strategic approach to selling a solution helps solidify a long-term relationship with the customer company. Figure 5-15 shows a pace diagram of how SlideShare fits into your preparation for a sales meeting.

When you are preparing the presentation for your sales meeting, your research should include searching on SlideShare for information about the target company's industry, as well as for competitive intelligence. Your slidedeck may contain information that can be obtained from other presentations, such as:

- Data and trends about the prospect's industry
- Competitive intelligence, including financial information if competitors are publicly traded companies
- Highlights from analyst reports
- Images and video about competitors
- Images and mock-ups or a demo of your product or service

Even if the prospect is aware of the information included in the presentation, including it demonstrates that the salesperson is knowledgeable about the space, and it creates common ground so everyone in the meeting is on the same page.

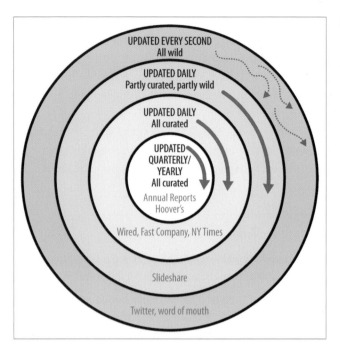

FIGURE 5-15
Use this pace layering diagram to show how SlideShare fits with other content marketing.

ENGAGE AND INTERACT IN THE MEETING

The meeting might be in person, or it might be conducted remotely. In either case, a visual presentation will ground the conversation, serve as a prompt for making sure all key points are covered, and provide a baseline for assumptions that can be validated or updated based on the discussion.

Prior to your meeting, ask if you can meet in a room with a projector and screen, so that you can play your presentation instead of being huddled around your laptop or tablet. Bring a VGA adapter, just in case you need it. If can't use a projector, that's OK. Make sure you're familiar enough with your slides that you can have a conversation and make eye contact with your prospects, and don't fix your eyes upon the computer screen.

In the world of insight selling, engaging and interacting with the customer is key.

FOLLOW UP AFTER THE MEETING

Follow up with a thank you, and send either a link to the presentation itself or a summary of the key points of your discussion, in presentation form. In a consultative role, the salesperson provides knowledge through carefully selected content. The visual presentation is your leave-behind, replacing the print brochures and pamphlets of pre-Internet times.

Make sure to watch the analytics on your SlideShare dashboard. You can track how many times your presentation has been viewed, and you can see if your prospects watched the entire presentation or if they stopped watching at a certain slide. This is valuable information for your follow-up conversations with them. It will also help you improve future sales presentations.

From prospect to lead to opportunity, presentations play a role in moving a potential customer through the sales process. Understanding the needs of each stage of the customer's progression is critically important to closing the sale.

Summary Tips

▸ Use LeadShare (with your PRO SlideShare account) to collect customer leads through the presentations, documents and videos you share on SlideShare.

▸ Activate LeadShare on a presentation to collect leads whether your slides are viewed directly on SlideShare or are embedded in an article or blog post on another website.

▸ If you have a Gold or Platinum account on SlideShare, you can target a specific geography in your LeadShare campaign.

▸ Always include a Call to Action (CTA) in your LeadShare form.

▸ Track the leads generated by your LeadShare campaigns using the PRO dashboard.

▸ Feed your LeadShare leads directly into SalesForce CRM by using Slide2Lead.

▸ Use SlideShare to research your prospect before your meeting. Show your slides during your meeting, and follow up with a thank-you note that includes a link to your presentation or to a summary of the key points of your discussion, in presentation form.

Research and Collaboration

IN TODAY'S COMPLEX, INFORMATION-RICH world, two skills rise to the top: research and collaboration. The more quickly you can find the information you need—and the more effectively you can put it to use—the better you and your company will fare.

Using SlideShare for Research

SlideShare is a great place to conduct research online because it is free, and the content is easy to find and share. How can you use SlideShare for research? We talked with some information professionals to find out.

Marcy Phelps, past president of the Association of Independent Information Professionals (AIIP) and owner of Phelps Research, uses SlideShare and recommends it as one of her favorite sources for business information. "It's great for picking up market statistics, identifying experts, and getting competitor insights," she says. Although she doesn't always find answers to specific questions, it is a valued tool in her toolbox.

Similarly, Ellen Naylor, former board member of the Strategic & Competitive Intelligence Professionals (SCIP) and CEO of the Business Intelligence Source, points out that SlideShare is a great way to stay up on what the competition is doing. "And it's a great way to learn as well," she adds.

For example, one of Ellen's colleagues, a librarian at a corporate library, was asked to explain the concept of *gamification* to an executive who didn't believe it was a real word. She went to SlideShare, searched for "gamification" (as shown in Figure 6-1), and found a few slidedecks that provided an excellent introduction and complete tutorial on the topic, such as Sebastian Deterding's "Meaningful Play: Getting Gamification Right."

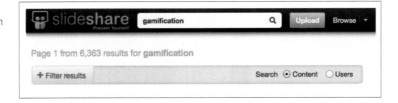

And SlideShare isn't restricted just to business topics. Teachers can also find excellent tutorials, such as the one on solar eclipses (*http://slidesha. re/14G9lhW*), as well as slides aimed at specific grade levels, such as a set of lessons on astronomy for eighth graders (*http://slidesha.re/V1xDjg*).

QUICKLY FIND RESULTS

The visual nature of slides makes them much more accessible as a way to learn about a topic that's otherwise dry. The visuals make it more interesting and, unlike a video, you can scan slides much more quickly and meaningfully to get just the information you need.

Let's walk through an example. Imagine you work in the pharmaceutical industry. You can enter a broad term, such as "pharma," into SlideShare's search bar and come up with more than 7,000 slidedecks. Or you can search for specific company names or specific product names.

You can also look for industry professionals. Presentations from industry insiders are particularly useful for in-depth analyses or discussions of trends. For example, Rachel Bates Wilfahrt, an analyst at the University of Denver, used SlideShare to identify the state of the art of social media use in pharma. Through SlideShare, she found *@pharmaguy*, aka John Mack, a pharma marketing pundit. His SlideShare presentations detail pharma's social media road map, chronicling its milestones as well as its mistakes.

[**TIP**]   **Find Related Content**

When you look at any deck on SlideShare, SlideShare automatically presents you with a list of slides that are related to that deck, in the appropriately named Related column. That's an efficient way to find additional information relevant for your research. What's more, once you've found particular users whose content you find useful, you can click the Follow button to receive automatic notifications whenever they upload a new presentation, document, or video.

KEEP UP WITH TRENDS

SlideShare is also a valuable source for trend analysis and research summed up in one place. The vast amount of information and data available today offers a constant stream of research conducted on almost any topic. Although websites and blogs are regularly updated with competitive information, market research, and the results of scientific inquiry and academic study, they often lack a thoughtful analysis that pulls together disparate information into a coherent whole. That's where turning to SlideShare is helpful: to get those insights in a format that's designed to be shared.

> **[TIP] Find Trends Quickly**
>
> At the end of every calendar year, industry leaders, analyst firms, and research organizations post presentations that summarize the previous year's trends and predict the upcoming year's hot topics. Use the search term "trends" and the year you're looking for to find these reports.

FOLLOW THOUGHT LEADERS AND RESEARCH REPORTS

Increasingly, thought leaders are using SlideShare as their destination for publishing research in the form of presentations. Researchers and analysts recognize that uploading presentations to SlideShare:

- Builds a body of knowledge
- Establishes their credibility as subject matter experts
- Creates an archive that demonstrates longevity in the subject

Viewers are hungry for well-informed trend analysis, such as the Internet Trends Report presented by Mary Meeker of Kleiner Perkins Caufield & Byers at the "D: All Things Digital" conference in New York City.

When you're looking for statistics, examples, trends, and concerns about today's business climate, SlideShare presentations provide the expert view you want. In the past, this type of information was available only for a fee. But leading firms now recognize the value in sharing information.

Rogers Communications, for example, is a Canadian provider of wireless, cable TV, home phone, Internet, media, and sports properties. Rogers recently commissioned a study on how connected Canadians are using the Internet now and how they want to use it in the future. Rogers published the complete study results on SlideShare.

A growing number of thought leaders are posting their analysis of trends as presentations on SlideShare. Even if the primary function of your company is not research, you can increase your reach and influence by sharing knowledge through presentations. Posting research on SlideShare increases the credibility of your company or organization and strengthens your brand. Research and analysis that is published on SlideShare creates an easily findable archive, a body of knowledge.

[TIP]   Expanding Your Network

You can expand your network by following presenters who upload and share content that interests you. When searching and browsing through SlideShare presentations, be sure to *favorite* those that you want to return to. New uploads from people you follow will appear in your SlideShare newsfeed.

Here are three examples of researchers who publish reports and analyses as presentations on SlideShare:

Altimeter Group

Altimeter Group is a research-based advisory firm whose business model includes sharing its research and analysis with the business community. Although the consultants at Altimeter publish information on the firm's website and the consultants' individual blogs, the central location for their reports is their SlideShare network.

Trendwatching

Trendwatching delivers trends, insights, and related hands-on innovations to over 160,000 business professionals in more than 180 companies. Each month, Trendwatching shares its latest findings in a free Trend Briefing. The slidedeck is uploaded to SlideShare, with links to more detail on the Trendwatching.com website.

MIT Sloan Management Review

The MIT Sloan Management Review recently shared its survey questions and responses from the 2012 Social Business Global Executive Study and Research Project, conducted with Deloitte, as shown in Figure 6-2.

Researchers surveyed more than 3,400 corporate leaders and conducted a series of in-depth interviews with experts and corporate practitioners to discover how social networking is transforming business. The slidedeck includes the detailed questions and responses, and the opening slide includes a link to the in-depth report on the MIT.edu website (*sloanreview.mit.edu/socialbusiness2012*).

FIGURE 6-2

MIT's Sloan School of Business shares its survey results in a presentation format on SlideShare.

DISCOVER A VARIETY OF RESOURCES

The sheer size of SlideShare makes it possible for you to find a variety of sources when researching a topic. Nongovernmental organizations (NGOs), from the Institute for the Study of War to the National Wildlife Federation, publish their findings as presentations. For example, a search on climate change results in presentations ranging from scientific institutes to universities to individual influencers, such as Andrew Revkin, author of the Dot Earth blog on the *New York Times* website.

If you're researching the effects of climate change on the United States, the EcoWest slidedecks will display in your search results. View one of EcoWest's presentations, and you'll see that it has a channel, shown in Figure 6-3. The channel contains slidedecks about specific topics related to climate change and environmental data.

FIGURE 6-3

Open a
presentation from
search results,
and you're likely
to discover entire
channels about that
topic.

Checking EcoWest's profile will let you know if it provides the type of information that will be helpful to your research. Browsing its presentations results in discovering a slidedeck that specifically addresses climate change in the US West and includes data about projected changes in precipitation, as shown in Figure 6-4.

If there are other presentations contained in a channel, you can "like" them as a way to bookmark them for future reference. You will probably want to follow EcoWest, so that any new uploads will display in your SlideShare newsfeed. As a follower, you'll also see when EcoWest "likes" or comments on a presentation from another SlideShare user. This is a great way to expand your network of research resources on SlideShare.

In addition to research reports, you'll find slidedecks and videos of presentations delivered at professional events. If the data found in research summaries needs more interpretation, search a little deeper for a conference or webinar where the findings might have been summarized and presented to an audience.

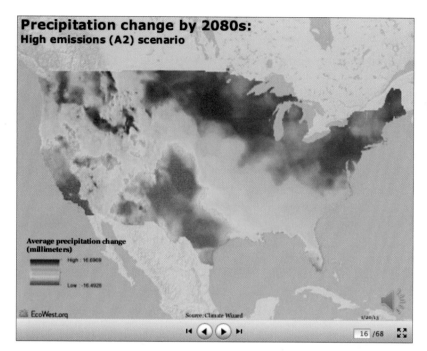

Precipitation change by 2080s:
High emissions (A2) scenario

Average precipitation change (millimeters)

High : 16.6909

Low : -16.4928

EcoWest.org   Source: Climate Wizard   1/20/13

16 /68

FIGURE 6-4

Explore specific presentations within a channel to find more detailed information in your research.

RESEARCH BEST PRACTICES

You can also use SlideShare to follow the evolution of a new best practice. In August 2010, Jeff Gothelf published a slidedeck outlining how The Ladders, where he was the director of user experience, was integrating user experience practice with an agile development environment. The presentation, "Beyond Staggered Sprints: Integrating User Experience and Agile," was the first in what became a series documenting the evolution of the concept known as *Lean UX*.

Less than a year later, with the practice of Lean UX stirring up an active dialogue within the design community, Jeff published on SlideShare his presentation *"Lean UX: Getting out of the deliverables business" (http://slidesha.re/eOOhin)*, which quickly became a manifesto for user experience professionals who were moving toward the agile movement (see the section "Incorporate Agile Development" later in this chapter for more details) that was gaining momentum in software development as a standard design process.

By May 2012, the best practices that Jeff and his team implemented led to a more specific definition of Lean UX. His SlideShare presentation *"Lean UX: Building a shared understanding to get out of the deliverables business"* (*http://slidesha.re/Klotp3*) created a common understanding about what the concept actually means.

In addition to research results, reports, and summaries, some presentations on SlideShare address methods and best practices for actually *conducting* research.

Michael Habib is a product manager and librarian who is passionate about creating intuitive user experiences that connect people with the information and experts they need. Michael shared his recent research in "New Technologies: Empowering the Research Community for Better Outcomes," a presentation that examines digital trends and their effect on streamlining scholarly literature research. One slide from his presentation, shown in Figure 6-5, illustrates the movement toward a *lean* approach to research, along with the reasons for this change.

FIGURE 6-5
Graphic depictions of trends can provide an overview of a topic.

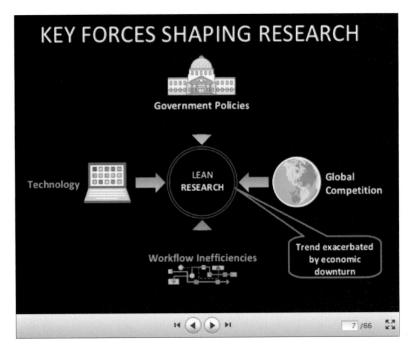

Michael uses graphs, quotations, and images to convey the trends that affect traditional research. He also includes recommendations for tools and resources that researchers should use. By using SlideShare to publish his presentation, Michael puts into action the very changes in research methodology that his presentation addresses.

Similarly, the Pew Internet & American Life Project aims to be an authoritative source on the evolution of the Internet, through surveys that examine how Americans use the Internet and how their activities affect their lives. The project generously shares its research, which spans from the shift of Americans' reading habits to a study of how young adults get news and information about their local communities.

RESEARCH CURRENT EVENTS

SlideShare is also a powerful resource for investigating recent events. Shortly after the devastating tsunami that hit Japan in 2011, the International Atomic Energy Agency (IAEA), a multidisciplinary agency headquartered in Vienna, Austria, began publishing reports on the radioactivity levels present at the Fukushima nuclear power plant. Between March and June 2011, IAEA uploaded more than 80 reports, providing updated data on the levels of radioactivity, as shown in Figure 6-6.

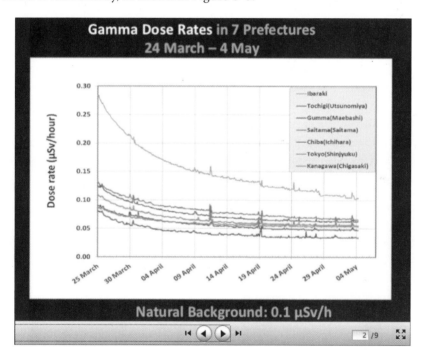

FIGURE 6-6
The IAEA provided weekly updates as presentations on SlideShare.

This presentation provides a single location for journalists, researchers, students, and public safety officials to find data and analysis of the risks at Fukushima, all available to download for free on SlideShare.

SHARE USER-GENERATED CONTENT

If you're looking for thoughtful content and images on events as they happen, go to SlideShare. At the time of this writing, Hurricane Sandy is fresh on our minds. The eastern seaboard of the United States is home to some of the largest news and media centers in the world. What happens when a catastrophic event such as Hurricane Sandy occurs? Those media hubs find themselves in the same predicament as the millions of citizens and businesses all along the affected area. Some TV news stations, such as CNN and MSNBC, were able to remain on the air, but their mobility was limited.

Christine Haughney and Brian Stelter reported in the *New York Times* on October 31, 2012:

> *Radio stations, one of the most reliable sources of information for people without power, were also impeded by flooding on Monday. Two news radio stations, WNYC and WINS, lost their AM frequencies but continued to broadcast on FM. WNYC's transmitter "is in a swamp, and it's flooded," said Laura R. Walker, the chief executive of New York Public Radio, which operates the station.*

Though some popular media outlets were down, the Internet was still up, and SlideShare has become a platform for publishing user-generated content during natural disasters and significant political and social events like this one.

We know from past international events, such as the flooding in Pakistan and the earthquake and tsunami in Japan, that SlideShare community members express their concern and support, as well as their expertise and knowledge, to help those affected by these events. This sharing also helps inform the greater community about the details, causes, and long-term outcomes affecting those who are involved, as shown in Figure 6-7.

FIGURE 6-7
A presentation by Kinvey.com shows how people shared information during superstorm Sandy.

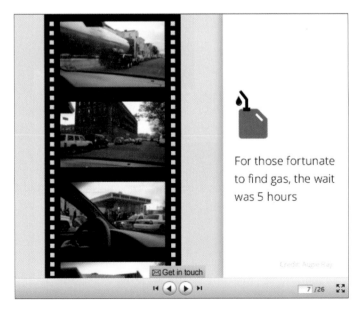

For those fortunate to find gas, the wait was 5 hours

In a matter of hours after the storm hit Florida, slideshows started appearing on the Popular section of SlideShare search results. Social sharing via the SlideShare community provides a crowd-sourced curation of images, uploaded as slideshows and shared with the world.

Research Summary Tips

▶ Follow your peers (or competitors) on SlideShare to keep up with what people in your industry are posting.

▶ Learn about a new product introduction.

▶ Get up to speed on a new topic by doing a keyword search on SlideShare.

▶ Use SlideShare in your research efforts to find market statistics and identify trends and best practices.

▶ If you have to learn about a new topic that you find dry or boring, look for some slideshows on it to lighten your cognitive burden with visuals.

▶ Use SlideShare's search and related content features to find subject matter experts.

▶ If you are a thought leader, publish your insights on SlideShare to establish credibility, demonstrate your portfolio of knowledge, and create an archive that demonstrates longevity in the subject.

▶ Slide presentations often summarize research and identify trends in a quick, easy-to-grasp way that's designed to be shared.

Using SlideShare for Collaboration

Every year, the Hay Group conducts a global Best Companies for Leadership survey. The most recent findings (by Rick Lash, National Practice Leader, Leadership and Talent) show that collaboration is necessary for companies to innovate and solve complex problems. Not surprisingly, however, most company leaders do not know how to collaborate effectively.

Part of the problem is that *collaboration* is not the same as *teamwork*. Collaboration must happen across functions and across units, which is where most companies drop the ball. Sony, for example, didn't come up with an MP3 player until three years after the iPod, because (as UC Berkeley professor Norten Hansen found after studying the company) Sony had a competitive culture, and a digital music player did not make much sense from a P&L standpoint for any individual business unit. So, the project stalled.

Why did internal competition at Sony result in the product getting stuck? It seems like common sense to say that teams will progress and be more productive when they collaborate instead of working against each other.

Michael Tomasello, author of *Why We Cooperate* (MIT Press), has researched human behavior to understand the motivations that people have for cooperating. He found that cooperation is a naturally occurring behavior in young children. It draws upon a sympathetic emotion that is not taught, but that is inherent in the emotional evolution of humans. The *we* intentionality results in cross-cultural robustness in societies and business. Sharing of ideas, helping each other, and building upon existing conventions is at the core of innovation.

COLLABORATE ACROSS GEOGRAPHIES

When consulting firm Booz & Company asked R&D leaders in 186 companies in 19 nations to name their top three challenges, the second largest challenge cited was how to encourage collaboration across geographic locations and functions.

How do firms tackle the challenge? Having a collaboration platform that everyone can access is important. Eloqua, a marketing automation company, saw SlideShare's potential in that way. "Eloqua is mostly a decentralized organization," says Joe Chernov, Vice President of Content Marketing at Eloqua:

> The biggest office is Toronto, executives are in Virginia, and our international hub is in London. We have regional offices in Germany and Singapore, and our best practices team is in Austin along with SVP of Sales. We use video conferencing a lot and social media is a real unifier. I'm going to use SlideShare as a hub for all the content that is "shareworthy." We'll upload the best of the best, because it's recent and curated to be sharable.

Collaboration platforms let people work together regardless of their physical location. What's more, using SlideShare as a collaboration platform lets you connect with others serendipitously—that is, you don't need to know whom to contact to get an answer; you can discover them, the way Rachel Bates Wilfahrt found expert John Mack. You simply go to SlideShare, search on a keyword of interest, and start exploring slides, related slides, and their creators, followers, and commenters.

The openness of SlideShare means that you can interact with customers and potential customers to get their feedback as well, including their voice in the process.

USE ZIPCAST TO COLLABORATE

Most teams find in-person, real-time collaboration to be the most productive and valuable way to work together. A synchronized work effort allows for greater intimacy and faster forward motion than when technology is inserted in between team members.

But we work in a world that increasingly consists of globally dispersed teams. Work may occur during the middle of the day for some of the team, while the rest of its members are sound asleep. This asynchronous collaboration requires tools and processes that are not compromised by the contributors' different time zones.

Zipcast (a free, ad-supported feature for basic users) allows team members in different locations to meet online with streaming video while playing a presentation during the meeting. The meeting organizer can schedule a Zipcast, invite participants, and select a presentation to display during the meeting, as shown in Figure 6-8.

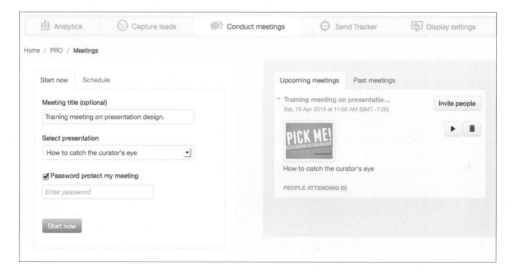

Because Zipcast is browser-based, participants don't have to download any software. In addition, it doesn't take over the entire screen, so users can leave other browser windows open. You can see the video (and hear audio) of the presenter who is also driving the slides. And everyone can chat.

Dr. Janet Corral, faculty member in Educational Informatics at the University of Colorado, uses SlideShare to collaborate with other medical educators. When working on an international open source project, Janet and her colleagues needed a way to communicate across universities in

FIGURE 6-8
Use Zipcast to engage in real-time online collaboration.

different countries. Janet used SlideShare to hold a private webinar, using SlideShare's Zipcast capability. Although some universities have private webinar tools, they're not always accessible, so SlideShare provides a way for people at different institutions to collaborate. With a SlideShare PRO account, you can restrict access of some of your slides to only a select group of PRO account holders.

"SlideShare is great for private presentations that need to go to a distributed group," Janet says. Although she could use Skype, "a Skype call becomes a Gong Show when people try to share," and using Google Hangouts in academia can be a hurdle. "Google is problematic in academia," Janet explains, because "institutions are not Google-friendly, so we need something that everyone can use," she says. "In SlideShare, we can create a private space to discuss the next steps of what we want to do, and then release it to a larger community," she concludes.

Using SlideShare, Janet and her colleagues can get feedback on their presentations privately, giving a preview to a small set of people and getting their comments. They can then refine their presentations before distributing them to a wider audience. Once each person is satisfied with his or her own presentation, she can make the presentation public with the click of a button.

USE SLIDESHARE AS A TEAM

At SlideShare, visual collaboration is essential to the company's ability to develop features quickly and iterate on existing products. Amit Ranjan, cofounder and CTO of SlideShare, uses SlideShare's own functionality to collaborate within the company.

According to Amit:

> Design mock-ups are done extensively using PowerPoint, then uploaded and shared with internal teams using a private URL. Much of our product literature, how-to guides, and demos are created in presentation form so they can be shared on the SlideShare platform. For collaborating during remote team meetings, we use Zipcast.

[TIP] Use SlideShare's Private Setting

The Private setting for SlideShare presentations comes in handy when sharing proprietary slidedecks. Much more secure than sending through email, this method also ensures that all viewers are viewing the same version. This is particularly useful for small businesses and professionals who don't use SharePoint, or a company-networked drive or document-sharing service such DropBox, for transferring files. Chapter 2 provides instructions for uploading a private presentation.

One of the things that makes PowerPoint a popular collaboration tool is that it is very modular. This allows members of a team to work on different topics concurrently. Separate modules of thought can be brought together like pieces of a puzzle to form a slidedeck. In addition, the boundaries of each slide provide constraints, forcing the user to be succinct. In *Speaking PowerPoint: The New Language of Business* (Insights Publishing), Bruce R. Gabrielle describes how the Hughes-Fullerton division of Hughes Aircraft used similar constraints to develop proposals for government contracts. Called STOP (Sequential Thematic Organization of Publications), this new method required that each topic in a proposal be presented as a "thought module" limited to 500 words contained on two pages. Bruce asserts that the STOP method—and thinking of slides as "thought modules"—is also a way to create clear and persuasive presentations.

In addition to brevity, PowerPoint can soften potentially acrimonious discussions during collaboration meetings. Bruce points out, "Everybody comes to a meeting with their assumptions. Debates and discussions can get personal. When you start to insert visuals into these debates, it makes the debate less controversial."

Instead of aiming the disagreement at other members of the group, point the discussion to the visual slides. This makes the discussion less personal, reduces confrontation, and increases collaboration.

[**REAL-WORLD EXAMPLE**] Sebastian Majewski of UN DESA

 Sebastian Majewski works at the United Nations Department of Economic and Social Affairs (UN DESA), an organization that helps countries around the world meet their economic, social, and environmental challenges.

Charged with a mission to "enable the world to make informed decisions," UN DESA turned to SlideShare to create a social media hub, the UN DESA Presentation Channel, to house its complex data and content—from statistical analysis and policy briefs to reports on global development conferences.

One of the United Nation's largest departments, UN DESA has 10 subdivisions, each structured by specialty, such as its Population Division, UN Statistics, or Social Policy and Development. Despite this large presence, many people don't know what UN DESA is. Like at many governmental organiza-

tions, the hierarchical structure was a hurdle for information dissemination.

So, UN DESA began searching for a social media channel that would work for its organization. "SlideShare was the tool that best fit our needs," Sebastian says, "since it has the interaction and integration, without the commitment of (managing) a Facebook page. We provide information to users and they can disseminate it for us, through sharing and embedding."

Starting with a single SlideShare channel, Sebastian worked with SlideShare's Business Development team to expand UN DESA's presence by creating multiple accounts with branded channels. Now, the UN DESA Presentation Channel serves as a hub for the other UN DESA division channels, which all have the same look and feel. UN DESA also decentralized its publishing process, which, Sebastian says, "empowers

each division by giving them control over their own content. We then take it and stream it on the parent channel." The SlideShare Network is also a time saver, because content owners can now direct user questions and requests directly to their SlideShare channels.

According to Sebastian, SlideShare also helped UN DESA improve the flow of internal communications by establishing "a strong culture of information sharing." After being trained to use their SlideShare accounts, content owners began uploading documents, subscribing to each other's channels, and coordinating with experts from other departments. ◆

INCORPORATE AGILE DEVELOPMENT

Projects of any kind need a process to keep them moving toward the desired end result. A number of traditional project methodologies have been used for many years, but to be competitive in an Internet marketplace, software development teams need to accelerate their development process.

In 2001, 17 software developers got together to redefine software development. They saw the need to break away from the time-consuming, highly structured waterfall project management process followed by the grandfathers of technology like IBM. This group defined what is now known as *agile software development*. The *Manifesto for Agile Software Development*, published soon after their meeting, includes "customer collaboration over contract negotiation" as one of its key tenets. The best practices of this new process have spread into businesses beyond software and technology. They can apply in almost any situation where project management is needed.

Throughout the agile process, communication and collaboration are critically important, both within the team and with the customer. But there is no time allotted to create lengthy text requirements and specs. In fact, documentation itself is secondary to creating working prototypes and code.

When speed and agility are required during the development of a business, product, or idea, written documentation can be slow and cumbersome. Visual designs are more efficient and accurate tools for capturing and communicating ideas:

- Visual collaboration levels the playing field, promoting a neutral culture of trust.
- Visual records create artifacts of collaboration, capturing the intentions and shared understanding of the participants.

Bill Scott is Senior Director of User Interface Engineering at PayPal and coauthor of *Designing Web Interfaces: Principles and Patterns for Rich Interaction* (O'Reilly). Bill leads user interface engineering (web development) for all of PayPal's customer-facing applications. Drawing from his previous experience at Yahoo! and then Netflix, Bill incorporates the most low-tech process possible when his team is designing and developing user interfaces. Bill has had much success with this approach to collaboration, and he speaks at conferences around the world, sharing his teams' experiences, as shown in Figure 6-9.

FIGURE 6-9
Bill Scott leads his
team at PayPal in
a low-tech, highly
iterative design
process.

As he and the PayPal development team worked on reinventing the checkout process in the spring of 2012, Bill set aside traditional tools and worked on a shared understanding of what the team needed to accomplish. The ideas needed to be communicated visually.

Here are Bill's three essential elements to creative collaboration:

Shared understanding

A shared understanding gets to the heart of the problem, reducing the need for text-based documentation.

Deep collaboration

Individual team members can break away only for short lengths of time. It's essential that all members come back quickly to the team.

User feedback

For usability, the design research team runs the sessions. The team includes engineers, product managers, and designers. They conduct research through interviewing and customer surveys.

A culture of trust is essential to successful agile development. There must be a company culture that makes it safe to make mistakes. In PayPal's case, CTO James Barrese wanted to encourage creative collaboration by creating a "skunkworks" environment where every voice was heard. Bill says that this executive-driven innovation is essential to rapid innovation: "If everybody feels like they're having an impact, it affects the creative juices of the team. The team doesn't focus on internal politics; they focus on outward results."

SKETCH IDEAS WITH A DESIGN STUDIO METHODOLOGY

An environment of collaboration is truly the keystone to a culture of innovation. This means designers must be included at the start of the project, not at the end when all of the problem definition and requirements gathering has already taken place. It also means that everyone on the team knows that they add value to the project. With the absence of text documentation, designers are the scribes for visually capturing ideas and feedback.

There is no time or space for design divas. In his *UX Magazine* article *"Introduction to Design Studio Methodology"* (*http://bit.ly/oudYTV*), Will Evans describes his philosophy this way:

> The reality of designing modern digital solutions is that no individual can solely capture all the complexity of creating a truly vibrant product with various customer engagement points, different usage patterns, and behaviors based on complex needs, goals, and customer backgrounds, all interwoven into an emergent, ubiquitous engagement tapestry. This is why innovation really is, and should be, a team sport. The Design Studio methodology provides a collaborative, pragmatic process of illumination, sketching, presentation, critique, and iteration, leading to a shared vision and hopefully a more coherent and elegant solution.

Ideas turn into sketches, which are presented, critiqued, and revised, as shown in Figure 6-10.

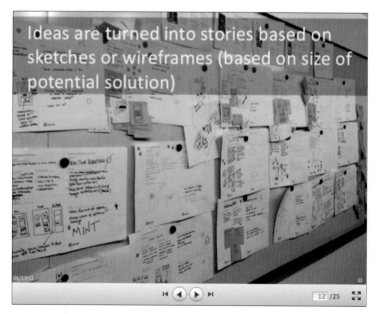

FIGURE 6-10
The design studio method welcomes everyone's comments and feedback.

During the presentation stage, sketches serve as the discussion platform from which designers and stakeholders debate their "preferred state and how to get there." The critique of sketches challenges assumptions and provides direction for the next iteration of design. More iterations follow, until only the strongest sketched design concepts survive.

DEVELOP PROTOTYPES RAPIDLY

The sketches evolve into *prototypes*, which are again critiqued and revised. Prototypes are not a deliverable at the end of a design process, but they are a necessary component to the iteration process described in the previous section. Ideally, the team includes a programmer who can start turning the sketches into working prototypes. Bill Scott (see the "Incorporate Agile Development" section) makes sure that the programmers and designers are in the room together, to expedite the creation of a coded, functional prototype.

In situations where a coder isn't available, PowerPoint and Keynote make iterative prototyping possible. Especially for small businesses, the availability of a programmer to code prototype designs is a luxury. In larger environments, the technical tools that provide polished prototypes can actually slow down the design process, an observation that Bill Scott made while at Yahoo. Plus, these tools can be too expensive for the budget of a startup or small business.

Both PowerPoint and Keynote support clickable hotspots, allowing the viewer to click and jump to other slides. This means web designers can create a slideshow as an interactive prototype, without actually coding up pages.

In his book, *Prototyping: A Practitioner's Guide* (Rosenfeld Media), Todd Zaki Warfel refers to prototyping as a common visual language, with which members of incongruous teams can understand each other and collaborate through visual design. Programmers may be more comfortable brainstorming in code, or marketers might prefer words. Visual prototypes create a neutral environment for collaboration and shared understanding.

As Todd says, "Once we shifted away from more static representation to something more interactive, it made a huge difference in the approach we took to design as well as the response we got back from clients." He recommends the use of sketchboards, where quick sketching of ideas can take place without the linear constructs of storyboards. For more information about creating prototypes, pick up a copy of Todd's book.

OVERCOME COLLABORATION KILLERS

Leaders face four challenges when trying to establish a collaborative culture:

- Silos with different existing cultures
- Strong egos and pontificators who don't listen to others
- Hidden agendas that may sabotage the collaboration
- Cynicism

To overcome these challenges, leaders need emotional intelligence. According to the July 2011 *Harvard Business Review* article "Bringing Minds Together," collaborative leaders are:

Passionately curious

They seek new insights and believe that others have these insights.

Modestly confident

They can bounce ideas off others without turning it into a competition.

Mildly obsessed

They care more about achieving the collective mission rather than how it will benefit their personal fortunes.

Collaboration, simply put, is about people working together to achieve a common goal. By applying several minds to a task, collaboration can improve the robustness and effectiveness of the outcome. But obstacles can get in the way of collaboration. For example, not knowing whom to contact for help or information can stifle collaboration. In addition, duplication of work (due to lack of communication or visibility) can also hurt collaboration and demoralize participants. Using SlideShare in your collaboration efforts can overcome these collaboration killers.

First, SlideShare helps you identify people who have the expertise to help you or have valuable information to share. Second, posting your work on SlideShare maintains visibility that reduces duplication of effort. As mentioned earlier, you can post work-in-progress privately on SlideShare, sharing your work only with your team members until it is completed. That way, your team can collaborate and see each other's progress while still keeping your work "under wraps" until it is ready to be made public or shared more widely.

Leaders can build a collaborative community in three ways:

- Inspire members with a vision of change that is beyond any of their individual powers to bring about.
- Convince members that the other collaborators are vital to the effort and are up to the challenge.
- Prevent one party from benefiting so much that the others feel their contributions are being exploited.

By posting your slides on SlideShare and embedding them on blogs, you extend the conversation and collaboration opportunities.

Collaboration Summary Tips

▶ Get comments on early drafts of your slides by releasing them privately to only a select group of people through a personal invitation. Get their comments and make refinements to your slides. When you're ready to launch, simply hit Public to publish your slides, ready for the world to see.

▶ Use Zipcast to hold a private webinar with your colleagues when collaborating on a project.

▶ If you're in a hierarchical organization, consider SlideShare as a way to improve the flow of internal communications.

▶ If you need to collaborate with colleagues across different geographies, consider making SlideShare a hub for all shareworthy content.

▶ Collaborate on content by sharing your slides on SlideShare. Embedding your slides in blog posts (and encouraging others to embed your slides in their posts) extends the conversation and commentary around your ideas.

Recruiting, Hiring, and Getting Hired

REGARDLESS OF YOUR PROFESSION and industry, the traditional résumé or curriculum vitae is alive and well. But here's what is new: your résumé versus online presence isn't an either/or situation. A full professional presence requires both. They complement each other and can be supplemented with a visual résumé and portfolio.

Your Traditional Résumé Belongs on Nontraditional Platforms

A quick way to get a hiring manager's attention is with data that reflects your success in previous positions. One way to get that attention is to depict your success visually. For example, provide a snapshot of that data with a bar chart or graph inserted as an image in your résumé. Don't be tempted to clutter it with detail. The goal is to provide an easy-to-read snapshot view of what you have achieved.

Winners of the Career Directors International Résumé Writing Contest demonstrate that a traditional résumé layout, primarily with text copy, is the preferred method for more traditional professional positions. Donald Burns won first place in the 2011 Toast of the Résumé Industry™ (TORI) résumé writing competition for his crafting of Jean-François Laurent's résumé. This traditionally formatted résumé included a small bar chart that is indicative of a growing trend. Even traditional résumés contain a visual quickie to catch the viewer's attention. By the way, Burns also won first place for Jean-François Laurent's LinkedIn profile.

In contrast, Cheryl Simpson, the winner of the Creative category, included bold borders and headlines and illustrations that demonstrated the job candidate Nina Leonetti's ingenuity and style.

Résumé and career coaches steer job candidates to focus on accomplishments instead of duties. If you've revised your résumé numerous times over the years, now may be the time to start from scratch. New energy, a quantifiable demonstration of your success, and a visual demonstration of your accomplishments will make your résumé stand out from the crowd.

Let's Get Visual

When it comes to searching for a new job, presentations are not just for public speakers. PowerPoint (and to a lesser extent, Keynote) is a household name. Think of all the accomplishments and experiences you've had during your professional life. Each one of these has value and a place in your story. Remember, the purpose of your traditional résumé is to create enough interest that a hiring manager contacts you for an interview. A presentation can increase that interest by giving a quick, visual representation of your story—hence the new term *visual résumé*.

A visual résumé can contain as little or as much information as you choose. Unlike a design portfolio, this new career tool illustrates your work history. It gives you the opportunity to tell your professional story. You can show excerpts from business documents, photos, drawings, or sketches that you may have created for a project. You may want to include photos of places you have worked, or where you have travelled on business.

Your visual résumé can include samples of your writing or programming code. Don't be afraid to add levity with a humorous slide or two. For example, Qualcomm employee Saranyan Vigraham had fun with his visual résumé (available online at *http://www.slideshare.net/saranyan/visual -resume*), relying on stock images as well as some of his own photographs to produce it, as shown in Figure 7-1.

FIGURE 7-1
Saranyan Vigraham tells his story with imagery.

Creative professionals can demonstrate their talent with engaging visual images, as Adam Kawilarang does in Figure 7-2.

FIGURE 7-2
A visual résumé lets you show your creative side.

An illustrated timeline provides a quick impression of how your skills have developed over time, as shown in the visual résumés by Pierre B. Gourde (Figure 7-3) and Hagan Blount (Figure 7-4).

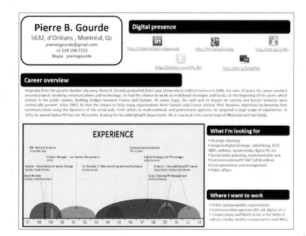

FIGURE 7-3
Pierre B. Gourde's timeline provides a visual glimpse of when specific work history occurred.

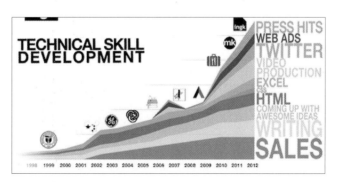

FIGURE 7-4
The strength of Hagan Blount's individual skills is conveyed by the font size.

Design Portfolio

Architects, artists, illustrators, web developers, muralists, urban artists, and curators are some of the professionals who could benefit from a design portfolio.

Abby Covert is an independent information architect working and living in New York City. In her workshop, "Everyone Needs a Portfolio," Abby advises that all professionals should show off their work with a portfolio:

> Whether you are a designer, a developer, a marketer, a student, or anything in between—in today's creative job market, every differentiator will count towards getting the job. Gone are the days of being able to talk over your future employer's head, just showing the latest deliverable you are working on, even worse showing nothing at all. Welcome instead to a world where your work is being measured not by what you say it was, but by what it really was.

Abby starts with a sketch, as shown in Figure 7-5, and then adds her one-line description of her professional identity.

FIGURE 7-5
Pull together
examples of your
work, and then
watch your portfolio
unfold.

Whereas the visual résumé tells the story of you and your professional life, the portfolio provides a visual demonstration of your strengths and accomplishments.

Four Locations for Your Résumé and Portfolio

Users with complete profiles are 40 times more likely to receive job opportunities through LinkedIn. Use the address book importer to import your address book directly from web-based email clients such as Gmail or Yahoo! Mail, or use the Outlook address book importer.

Once you've updated your profile, you're ready to add a presentation from SlideShare. If you're not a public speaker, that's OK. You can pull together information about your accomplishments, skills, and employment history to make a short presentation in PowerPoint or Keynote.

As shown in Figure 7-6, you have:

- A traditional résumé, in case it's requested
- A LinkedIn profile, so you can be found by hiring managers, recruiters, and other LinkedIn members
- A presentation that serves as a visual résumé of your career
- A portfolio presentation that displays your creative work

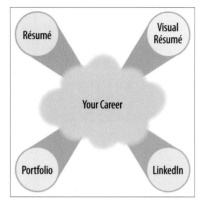

FIGURE 7-6
Be sure to have your career represented in these four formats.

Premium SlideShare account holders have the option of displaying one or all four presentations in their profile. If you are prolific in your presentations, you may want to include all four. If your goal is to draw attention to one message, then as a SlideShare Pro member you can display that one presentation that you want to make sure the hiring manager sees.

[**TIP**] **Rock Your Interview with a Visual Presentation**

When you are invited to interview for a specific position, make sure you bring a visual presentation in addition to your visual résumé or portfolio. The presentation should specifically address the open position, the company, and how you bring your knowledge and experience to hit the ground running in this role. Bringing a short presentation also demonstrates your ability to communicate above and beyond what the interviewers expect.

Since the use of visual communication in business is increasing, by bringing a presentation to your interview you will make a memorable impression and show you are up to speed on current communication trends.

When you share SlideShare content in the LinkedIn Update Stream, your connections can immediately view and engage with that content by clicking on a link or thumbnail, all without having to leave the LinkedIn site. That's a powerful way to keep you in front of connections and potential job networking leads. The benefit of having a résumé created as part of your LinkedIn profile is that there is only one place to update, which reduces the risk of outdated versions getting shared.

Continue your conversation online. Add to your LinkedIn connections. Include your LinkedIn and SlideShare URLs on your business cards.

Insights from Career Coach Jason Alba

 Jason Alba is the founder of Jibber Jobber, an online "personal relationship manager for your career." Jason started Jibber Jobber in 2006 when he was laid off from his position in IT. He realized that there was a huge gap between what was needed by professionals managing their careers and what was available.

Why should people who don't do public speaking add a presentation to their SlideShare and LinkedIn profiles? "It has nothing to do with public speaking, it's all about personal brand," job search coach Jason says. "No matter who you are, you should have a SlideShare presentation on or about you."

"It's OK to reuse everything on your LinkedIn profile," Jason goes on to say. "If you have cool visuals and I'm in a hurry, I can click through a presentation quickly. Your résumé in presentation form is a visualization of the brand message you're conveying on your profile."

Jason recommends that job seekers have a presentation on LinkedIn in order to keep the potential hiring manager engaged. "Go where your audience is and don't make them go anywhere else," he says.

Jason is an advocate for only displaying one presentation, in order to keep the hiring manager's attention. "You can easily send them to your SlideShare account to see

all of them if you want to...but from your LinkedIn profile, point people to where you really want them to go to without adding too many choices, confusion, or noise."

The visual web has had a direct effect on how people network when looking for a new job. "Pinterest has affected how we surf pages," Jason adds. "We were already skimmers and scanners. Job seekers are told that recruiters will spend 10 seconds looking at a résumé. We're taking normal-sized paragraphs and breaking them down to small paragraphs. We're consuming visual chunks of information."

A common mistake that Jason sees is an over-focus on recruiters:

> *Job seekers are mistakenly spending too much time trying to attract recruiters. With LinkedIn, there's a greater possibility of getting directly in front of the hiring manager. A hiring manager will take more time to go through a job candidate's profile and watch his or her SlideShare presentation.*

What's more, don't wait to post presentations until you're looking for a job; start now. It's appropriate to post presentations even if you're

gainfully employed. "Absolutely!" Jason encourages. "This concept is gaining acceptance as more and more people are taking control of their careers. People are still concerned about something happening to their jobs because they see people get laid off left and right. People are concerned because they know their jobs won't last forever, even at the executive level."

Jason recommends that all job seekers create a blog. It can be a bit intimidating to come up with new articles on a regular basis. Instead, create a few presentations, then embed them in blog posts. Tweet about each new blog post, and share it to targeted LinkedIn Groups. By sharing it with existing LinkedIn Groups, you don't have to create and build up a huge group of your own. LinkedIn Answers and Groups are two of the most important places to spend your time.

Above all, Jason advises, "Out of all the applications that are on LinkedIn, SlideShare is the must-do for everybody. If you have a LinkedIn profile, you should have a SlideShare presentation." ◆

Build Your Network with the Power of Weak Ties

In his book, *The Start-up of You* (Crown Business), LinkedIn founder Reid Hoffman explains how "it takes a network" to build your career. There are tiers of relationships within your professional network, and it pays to be thoughtful about how you nurture and utilize the individuals in each tier. Most of us have a small group of trusted friends and colleagues whose opinions we respect and whom we help and support unconditionally. These are our allies. As Hoffman describes it, these are the people with whom you proactively share and collaborate.

The next tier of your network is composed of acquaintances, the looser connections that Hoffman refers to as *weak ties*. You run into weak ties occasionally at conferences or events. You might know some of them only online. They aren't in your inner circle, so their networks stretch beyond your horizon. You have just enough in common to understand each other's position, but are far enough away to see from a different perspective.

If you rely only on your close allies to expand your network, you'll keep running into the same people. The power of weak ties lies in their diversity. Weak ties provide variation. Interestingly, these weak ties are best positioned to connect you with introductions that can expand your career, and with your public speaking opportunities.

"Weak ties in and of themselves are not especially valuable; what is valuable is the breadth and reach of your network," Hoffman explains.

The tier of weak ties provides not only a wider pool of connections, but also diversity as you seek inspiration for your presentations, both in design and content. It is in our nature to look for variation in the world around us. This very basic biological trait is the secret to creating captivating presentations, the slideshows that audience members talk about and give rave reviews. Variation also inspires creative thinking, new ideas that will get noticed by your network by keeping you out of the echo chamber.

"Relationships matter because the people you spend time with shape who you are and who you become," Hoffman adds. Your professional network is a community that requires interaction to stay alive and well. An effective way to keep your network healthy is to contribute to its members. Share information, and provide feedback and input when needed.

A powerful way to give to individuals in your network is to share presentations. There is so much valuable content in the form of research, best practices, case studies, and general information captured in the presentations on SlideShare. Seasoned networkers continually send links to presentations to members of their networks. This is an easy and thoughtful way to give while asking for nothing in return.

[REAL-WORLD EXAMPLE]   ## Jesse Desjardins

Jesse Desjardins, head of social media at Tourism Australia, explains how he landed that position by leveraging SlideShare. "Last year I was working at an ad agency in Paris and my contract was about to end," he says. "Instead of applying for another job I just put up some presentations on SlideShare in my spare time to see who was out there. I didn't really know what the outcome would be, but it seemed the more I posted, the more doors opened."

A conference organizer saw Jesse's slides and contacted him, asking if Jesse could do some social media and presentation work in Jordan and South Africa. "I jumped on that," he said.

Jesse enjoys traveling, and he traveled extensively during those six months. What's more, he continued to post his slides on SlideShare as he traveled (Figure 7-7). "People would find me through SlideShare and offer me projects to work on," Jesse says.

His presentations attracted further attention and were embedded on people's blogs (Figure 7-8).

"A few of my presentations got posted on popular blogs like Lifehacker and then things got a bit crazy from that moment on," Jesse says:

In May, I was asked to speak at a tourism conference in Australia and when I arrived in the country there was an opening at Tourism Australia to be the social media manager. It ticked all the boxes and I knew that it was exactly what I wanted. It's a government organization so I sent in my standard c.v. and then put up a visual version on SlideShare and tweeted it out once. Overnight, it was seen by a few thousand people.

Not only did Jesse showcase his talents, but his social network and the credibility he'd gained through SlideShare went to work for him as well:

People who had been watching my presentations for a while wrote some really nice comments with their endorsements. The next morning someone who worked for Tourism Australia saw it. He had been following me on

Twitter and forwarded my presentation to the entire office and executive team. I was called in for an interview that morning, and few days later I got the job.

Jesse's story is emblematic of others who have used SlideShare to showcase their talents and demonstrate their expertise. The wide audience that SlideShare attracts, as well as its integration to LinkedIn, means that your presentations get in front of not only recruiters and hiring managers, but also the very people who work in the companies where you want to get hired. Your presentations attract their attention, and they start following you. As happened with Jesse, these followers can be in a position to put you in touch with the decision makers and help you land the job. ◆

FIGURE 7-7
Use your own photos of places you visit to make presentations more personal.

FIGURE 7-8
Unexpected messaging and images capture viewers' attention.

Your Public Speaking Strategy

Many professionals include public speaking as part of their career strategy. Speaking at conferences and private events generates an income stream and encourages greater visibility to your work. It can lead to interviews, writing engagements, and future speaking opportunities.

Public speaking is not a requirement for growing your professional network and reputation, but for people who depend on increasing the size of their professional network, public speaking provides an effective way of reaching many people in much less time than contacting them one by one. What's more, you'll gain the benefit of serendipity of who might be in the audience to hear you. Furthermore, with the live streaming and replay of your presentation, your audience continues to grow even after the event has ended.

If you've wondered how seemingly unknown professionals in your field start popping up at one conference after another, it's not a mystery—it's a system. This system consists of three important steps that are repeated throughout one's speaking career: positioning, preparation, and presentation.

POSITIONING

To paraphrase Abraham Lincoln, "you can't speak at all of the conferences all of the time." And you really wouldn't want to speak everywhere anyway. A more efficient strategy, both for time and your own mental energy, is to think about the type of event or group where you would like to speak.

Do some searching online to find out who is most active in that group or venue, and then get to know them on social networks. If they are local, plan to meet them at the next get-together. You're not asking for anything, you're just learning more about this group or event. After a while, you'll begin to filter out the events and groups that aren't the short list of who and what you'd like to be associated with. This is how you position yourself professionally.

Go back and take a look at your LinkedIn profile. Does it contain some of the key words and descriptions of the direction you're taking? Make a few updates. Just like the classic advice, "dress for the job you want," positioning yourself in the group or sector that you want to be associated with requires thought, research, and action.

PREPARATION

Start gathering your thoughts about what kind of presentation you could create that would be interesting to people who are involved in this topic. Jot down your ideas and gather some illustrations and images like we talked about earlier. Research the Meetup groups that will connect you to the thought leaders and active participants in that field (see the section "Ease into Public Speaking with Meetup" later in this chapter). Connect to members on LinkedIn. Reach out and contribute to the community on social networks, and comment on the shared content.

As you attend or watch online, notice which elements of the presentation resonate with the audience or viewers. Take note of the design style, the pace, and the rhythm with which a presenter keeps your attention. Be thinking about how much humor is appropriate for this group or event. What is the vernacular, what are the hot terms and phrases that are receiving attention and deserve further research? Strong presenters are not only knowledgeable about their content, but they have also researched and are aware of who their audience is.

PRESENTATION

Take the leap, and present yourself! As you build a larger and larger audience over time, your professional network will increase in size. Once you're comfortable (at least enough to present again), circle back to your positioning and goals. Are you on track with where you set out to be? Do you need to adjust your expectations a bit? That's OK. Your career path is a work in progress; it's OK to be flexible.

As you tweak your positioning, always be thinking about what you need to do to prepare for the next presentation. Review feedback to gauge the receptiveness from the audience or viewers. Make adjustments for the next iteration of your presentation. Or start from scratch with a new topic or perspective. The main thing to remember is that this three-step process is exactly how popular presenters keep getting the gigs and how they move forward within the groups among whom they want to be known.

Seasoned "networkers" include this kind of connecting as an ongoing part of their career strategy. By using the same methods and behaviors they use, you can make it part of your public speaking strategy as well.

[REAL-WORLD EXAMPLE] ## Amber Case

Amber Case is an entrepreneur who studies the intersection of technology and human behavior. Amber focuses on the ways that technology can help people without getting in their way, a discipline she calls *cyborg anthropology*. A prolific writer and speaker, Amber has presented at TED, was a keynote speaker at SXSW 2012, and has spoken at conferences in Europe and Asia. Amber is 26 years old.

Amber credits her high school speech and debate experience with giving her the knowledge and confidence to speak in front of a crowd. The practice she got when competing in intramural debates gives her the ability to turn on a dime when the audience isn't reacting. Amber likens this skill to that of the gypsies, who would come into a town, gauge the audience in just a few minutes, and determine what to adjust in their acts. She is also confident taking questions from the audience. But all of this experience didn't automatically bring her speaking invitations, so she went after them.

Using the aforementioned tactics, Amber positioned herself in the line of sight for events. She planned ahead and gave her attention only to events that addressed her area of focus: technology and the human experience. She started locally, giving a presentation at the Inverge event in Portland, Oregon, where she lives. In the audience was a vice president at Disney, who was running the Creative Convergence Conference. She approached him with this value proposition: "You need a young person to speak at your conference." She heard nothing for weeks, and then, at the last minute, a scheduled speaker had to cancel. The VP called Amber and invited her to speak for 5 minutes, but she asked for 10 minutes and got it.

Always strategic, Amber used Twitter to reach the extended, off-site audience during her talk. She made sure each slide she used had fewer than 140 characters of text, so it could be easily retweeted (see Chapter 3). Amber tweeted "be sure to follow me so you can get information live from the conference." She asked a friend to sit in the back of the room and tweet each slide with the event hashtag. Her goal was to get the maximum exposure from social media in the 10 minutes that she had on stage.

Not only did she achieve the goal of increasing her reach beyond the conference, but her presentation was covered by the *Portland Business Journal* as well. This led to an invitation to speak at an event where the keynote speech would be given by someone from MIT. Amber had already set a goal to speak at MIT before she reached the age of 27, so this connection was just what she needed to make that happen. Sure enough, the keynote speaker got wind of her talk and invited her to speak at the Futures of Entertainment conference at MIT.

Soon after that came SXSW 2010, where her presentation was scheduled for a room that was off the main flow of traffic at the conference. Given how far the room was from the main venue, only the people most interested in Amber's topic attended. As she tells it, "There were only a hundred people in the room, but they were all nerdy so they understood my talk and gave it great reviews." These great reviews, coupled with Amber continuing to grow her audience and staying on track with her speaking goals (which included speaking at TED), gained her the coveted SXSW keynote address in 2012, as shown in Figure 7-9.

Here are Amber's tips for creating a public speaking presence as part of your personal brand strategy:

▶ Position yourself correctly and plan which events to target as your public speaking goals.

▶ View the slidedecks and videos of presenters you like, and develop your own personal style.

▶ Find the leaders in your discipline—the people who know everyone or are the keepers of the knowledge—and get to know them. In the process, they'll get to know you and will help bring you into the community.

▶ Learn the language of the community and connect with the people, in person as well as online.

▶ Get to know the people who have spoken at the specific events where you'd like to speak. These people are the connectors who can facilitate introductions and help you get speaking invitations.

The value of speaking in public is the visibility and credibility it brings, which can help your career tremendously. "Being a speaker is the most efficient way to meet everyone in the room," Amber says. They'll get to know you and remember you. Putting your slides on SlideShare provides a way to keep in touch, leverages what you created, and extends it to the broader audience worldwide. ◆

FIGURE 7-9
Amber Case's public speaking strategy landed her the coveted SXSW keynote in 2012 (photo by Kris Krug).

Create Your Presentation Personality

When it comes to creating presentations as part of your career strategy, it's wise to think like the marketing companies of major brands. In the same way that companies like Apple and Coca-Cola have recognizable typography and design essence, you can define the perception you'd like to convey by choosing a consistent design style and sticking to it.

With sites like TypeKit, you don't have to hire a branding agency to create character for your presentations. An inexpensive subscription allows you to browse and select the font that's right for you. Even if you are an employee of a company that has its own style, the presentations that you create outside of company work are your own and should reflect your professional personality. Sometimes just creating your name in a unique font can be the beginning of your presentation design style.

Your presentation, including your visual slidedeck, should provide an enriching experience for your audience. Will you be using photographs, illustrations, or data visualizations in your slides? Make sure that they are treated consistently, and that your choice of images has a flow to it. Slidedecks that have a distinctly different design style for each slide leave the audience feeling disjointed, giving the impression that your thoughts are held together by duct tape. A smoothly designed slideshow leads your audience from the beginning to end while you tell the story of your topic.

How do you come up with your own distinctive style? Don't worry if you don't know what it'll be right from the start. You can develop it as you go along. That's what Tara Hunt, CEO and cofounder of Buyosphere, did: "It was the combination of the Picasso quote that 'great artists steal' and the advent of SlideShare that made me into a professional public speaker." Hunt adds:

> My favorite thing about the sharing culture of the Web is that we can learn from one another's mistakes and successes. I started following some of my favorite speakers of all time and initially emulated their style.

Emulation gave Hunt a chance to practice, giving her something concrete to follow as she learned the ropes. Throughout her development as a public speaker, she shared her progress, ups, and downs (Figure 7-10).

"I borrowed styles liberally from everyone I loved, such as Kathy Sierra and Lawrence Lessig," Hunt says. "Then I'd post my finished product to SlideShare. With each iteration, I started to come up with my own personal presentation style until I felt 100% comfortable in my own skin."

FIGURE 7-10
Tara Hunt shares
her lessons learned,
encouraging other
speakers through
trial and error.

Visit Hunt's profile on SlideShare and you'll see what she means: "The evolution is apparent through my SlideShare history. Sometimes I love just going back and seeing how far I've come."

Ease into Public Speaking with Meetup

Even if you're not a public speaker and never intend to be, speaking in public is a very effective way to build your career and get noticed. Here are some ways to ease into presenting yourself in front of an audience.

As mentioned in Chapter 3, your first speaking gigs can be local, in front of small groups of people, and you probably won't be paid. That's OK and is to be expected. If you're not sure where to start, take a look at the Meetups in your area. Meetup.com allows you to search for groups who meet in person at a designated time and place to discuss and learn about specific topics. Pick the topics of interest to you. Then join a few of these Meetup groups and attend some Meetups, and you'll start to get a feel for each group's purpose and character.

Some Meetups are formal and follow an agenda, while some are more social and provide a great place to network. Many do both. As you get a feel for the Meetup group's vibe and level of expertise, you'll start to think of topics that may interest the group. Exchange business cards and contact information with the group's members and get their feedback on speaking ideas that you may present to the group. Usually, the organizers of a Meetup group are on the lookout for volunteer speakers, so be sure to connect with them as you attend the Meetups and get to know the group.

Attending Meetups also lets you get to know other professionals in a specific area of interest. This is a great way to build your network by contributing, sometimes just by showing up! For more introverted professionals,

Meetups are less nerve-racking than pure networking events, because everyone is there to learn and discuss a topic, not just promote themselves to strangers. You're free to participate as little or as much as you're comfortable with. In addition, as you get to know the Meetup group members, you'll hear about professional opportunities that may interest you. This is why *U.S. News and World Report* listed Meetup.com as one of the Top 8 Sites for Networking.

Not a Public Speaker? You Still Need Presentations

As mentioned earlier, everyone should have presentations included in his or her career strategy, not only when looking for a new job, and not only for public speakers. Presentations position you as having a certain level of expertise and can put you in a desired niche as a subject matter expert. Many presentations on SlideShare were never meant for the big screen or an auditorium. They are meant to be viewed by anyone interested in the topic or the content creator. Presentations let your peers know that you are up to speed on current information and trends. They also get the attention of people you would like to add to your network.

For example, Luis Suarez, a knowledge manager at IBM, has a SlideShare profile under his name that's on the IBM Network page. He's uploaded 16 presentations and 7 documents to date. He posts slides from presentations he's given, and he also has a quick-win strategy: he captures his live tweets from conferences he's attending and then posts them as a document on SlideShare. That strategy has served him double duty, garnering him not only real-time exposure on Twitter but also long-term across time and space on SlideShare.

If you have never created a presentation before, start small. Pick a topic that you care about and jot down some important points about that topic. Look through your own images or find some free or inexpensive images from stock image websites. Open a new PowerPoint or Keynote file and create a few slides. Add your key points as text, the information with the images. There you have it! When you upload it to SlideShare, be sure to share it on your social networks. This is the quickest way to create some buzz around your presentation.

If you already have a blog, write a brief introduction of why this topic is worth thinking about and embed your presentation into the blog post. Now you have a presentation on SlideShare, plus a multimedia blog post on your own site!

Why is this important to your career development? The exercise of creating a presentation forces you to think differently about a topic you are already familiar with. You have to think visually, and with brevity. It keeps you fresh with the topic and lets your network know that you are actively involved in the subject matter. The feedback you receive will help reduce the awkward feeling of exposure as you become more comfortable creating and sharing presentations.

When members of your network upload a presentation or embed one on their blog, be sure to comment on it and share it. This engagement with their content will encourage them to notice yours, and you'll receive comments and shares back in return.

Summary Tips

▶ Create a visual résumé that showcases your skills and experience through visual elements, such as photos and graphs. Upload it on SlideShare.

▶ Embed a graph or chart into your traditional résumé to make it stand out.

▶ Consider creating a design portfolio (if applicable to your profession) that provides a visual demonstration of the breadth of your work.

▶ Include presentations in your LinkedIn profile.

▶ Bring a presentation to your job interview, tailored to that job. This demonstrates preparation and superior communication skills.

▶ Build your network with looser connections (the *weak ties* beyond your closest colleagues) who have wider access to contacts outside your inner circle and can reach more people during a job search.

▶ Consider public speaking as part of your career strategy (regardless of whether you want to be a public speaker or not).

▶ Position yourself to speak at conferences in the field in which you want to be known.

▶ Ease into public speaking by presenting at Meetup groups.

▶ Create a distinctive presentation design personality.

▶ Demonstrate your subject matter expertise by creating slides in your field and sharing them on SlideShare.

Organizational Outreach and Communication

MUCH OF THE ADVICE about presentation design and delivery in this book is aimed at established, for-profit companies. But there are other types of organizations that can use presentations to achieve their business, outreach, and communication goals. What's more, these different organizational types face challenges unique to them. This chapter will examine those specific needs.

First, *startups* have many of the same challenges as established companies, but they have a few additional challenges that warrant special attention. In many cases, the startup founders are looking for investors; this means they need to be ready at any given moment to deliver a pitch presentation. Furthermore, pitch presentations face a high-stakes rigor unlike other presentations. We'll delve into those requirements in this chapter, to help entrepreneurs deliver winning presentations.

Second, *nonprofits* need to craft their message to present to each type of stakeholder (supporters, donors, foundations, partners, volunteers), all the while fulfilling their mission.

Third, *journalists* must address their careers as an independent freelancer might. Successful journalists have discovered the power and importance of building a following using social media.

Finally, *government agencies* are tasked with making sure they reach the greatest number of constituents possible, especially when asking for public input. They also want to make sure that citizens are aware of the resources and benefits the agency offers.

Let's take a look at how each of these groups can use presentations in their content and audience growth strategies.

SlideShare for Startups

The recent attention on entrepreneurship has led to the launch of thousands of startup companies in almost every business sector. The competition for obtaining investment funding is fierce. As a result, startup incubators and accelerators have sprung up all over the world.

The terms *incubator* and *accelerator* are often used interchangeably, given that both entities focus on helping entrepreneurs in the early stages of developing their companies. The primary difference between the two is that accelerators offer short, focused programs (usually just a few months), whereas incubators can nurture companies for years. The goal of both is to help startup founders understand how to assess the viability of their business idea, understand its market potential and risks, prepare them for pitching their business to potential investors, and make sure that they know how to get new customers.

YCombinator is the Harvard of startup accelerators (although it eschews the term), because it was the first (founded in 2005) and its graduate firms have the largest market value—$7.78 billion as of April 2012, according to *Forbes* (*http://onforb.es/IoNR1X*). YCombinator was followed by many other accelerators, including 500 Startups, TechStars, and Startup Weekend.

Accelerators and incubators are a valuable resource for entrepreneurs and are important in the context of this chapter because of the role that slide presentations play in these programs. Specifically, every startup accelerator program ends with a *demo day*, also known as a *showcase* or a *pitch event*. The purpose of demo day is to secure additional funding for the startup, and a key part of succeeding at demo day is having the right kind of slide presentation.

To explain this more fully, consider the example of Dave McClure, founder of 500 Startups. Dave is a serial entrepreneur and has taken his startup accelerator worldwide. Through 500 Startups, Dave provides early-stage companies with up to $250,000 in seed funding and a three-to-six-month intensive "startup bootcamp" that includes mentors and designers in residence. In 2012, Dave created Startup Village at the South by Southwest (SXSW) Interactive Festival, bringing together successful entrepreneurs, coaches, investors, and advisors for a conference within a conference at the annual event in Austin, Texas.

DEMO DAY AT 500 STARTUPS

The companies chosen to participate in the 500 Startups accelerator have a wide variety of business ideas. At the end of the three-to-six-month program, founders are required to give a live pitch presentation about their company, accompanied by a slideshow presentation.

500 Startups takes full advantage of SlideShare by having each startup participant upload its slideshow prior to the Demo Day live presentations.

The presentations are set to "private" until the start of the demo pitches, when the slideshows are changed to "public." The 500 Startups SlideShare channel aggregates the demo day pitch presentations, as shown in Figure 8-1, making it easy for the media and potential investors to find them.

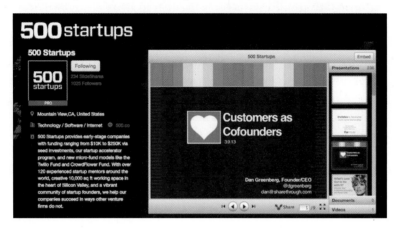

FIGURE 8-1
500 Startups publishes demo day presentations on its SlideShare channel.

Each presentation is specific to the business model, style, and *ask* (that is, the type of funding the startup is seeking), but all the presentations include the key elements found in a pitch presentation:

- Problem definition
- Proposed solution and story of how it came about
- Current customers and revenue (if any)
- Revenue model
- Description of the team
- Amount already raised (if any)
- Size of potential market
- Amount of funding sought

Dave advises all startup companies to focus on the problem and on how their product or service can make customers happy. The key is to emphasize the company's strengths and what advantages the company has over others in the same market. Have a plan for how you'll market your product, Dave suggests, and get your message out. Put the most important information on your first slide, and make sure it is memorable.

Since its inception in 2010, 500 Startups has amassed over 200 pitch slideshows on SlideShare of its graduates. This archive is a valuable resource for other startups looking for inspiration for the slideshows, and what investors are looking for in new companies.

STARTUP WEEKEND

Startup Weekend is part incubator and part *hackathon* (an event in which programmers collaborate intensively on a software project). In short, it's a 54-hour event in which developers, designers, marketers, product managers, and startup enthusiasts come together to share ideas, form teams, and build products in the hope of launching a startup.

These weekend-long, hands-on experiences take place all over the world, with local organizers pulling them together at a very low cost. On average, half of Startup Weekend's attendees have technical or design backgrounds, while the other half have business backgrounds. Unlike the accelerators that span weeks or even months, a Startup Weekend is a three-day race to the finish.

Startup Weekend was started in 2007 by Andrew Hyde, who was then working at the newly launched TechStars accelerator in Boulder, Colorado. In Startup Weekend's original format, each person who had an idea for a startup would present the idea on Friday evening. Having heard all the ideas, other participants would then choose the ideas that they were most passionate about and form a team. The teams immediately got to work writing code and developing a working prototype of the idea. At the end of the weekend, they presented a pitch slideshow presentation to the group, as shown in Figures 8-2 and 8-3. The focus was very much on the working prototype.

FIGURE 8-2
Startup Weekend ends with each team presenting a pitch (photo by Walkin Photos).

FIGURE 8-3
Startup Weekend
Seattle Women
participants pose
for the camera
(photo by Kyle
Kesterson).

Within a year, however, the *lean startup* movement arrived. "Eric Ries's blog changed everything," says Andrew. "The focus shifted to customer development." Instead of focusing on the *technology*, Andrew began to have Startup Weekend participants focus on the *problem* they were trying to solve. Instead of starting the Friday night kickoff with solutions, Andrew had them tell the story of a problem. Greater emphasis was placed on talking to the customer, feeling empathy with the problem, and telling the customers' stories.

Instead of trying to be the next billion-dollar "paradigm-shift" company, Startup Weekend teams focused on understanding the customer's needs and iterating based on the concepts described in Ries's book *The Lean Startup* (Crown Business).

"Most startups are about tinkering," Andrew says. "They aren't doing a paradigm shift. The problem statement has become more important, which was really exciting. Getting people on board with the problem more than the solution was a big change." He continues, "Putting the emphasis on the problem changed the story that the startups told."

What's the most important part of an effective pitch presentation? "Tone," says Andrew:

> The style of the pitch really matters. Be considerate of people's time. A pitch needs to get the audience to buy into the problem. Tell the story and be sure not to leave anyone behind. The takeaway needs to be memorable. Know your audience; know the room. Like they say in Outward Bound, be humble, yet bold.

Guy Kawasaki's handbook, *The Art of the Start* (Portfolio), aimed at "anyone starting anything," is a must-read for any startup or small business. Guy's now-classic "10/20/30 rule" has kept pitches on track for almost a decade:

- 10 slides
- 20 minutes
- 30-point-font text

The incubators described earlier in this section will probably give a pitch much less than 20 minutes, but the time limitation helps keep the presentation focused. Similar to Dave McClure's advice, Guy tells startup founders to "explain yourself in the first minute." The reason? You have only about one minute to capture their attention. He recommends these 10 slides for an investor pitch:

Title

Organization name, your name and title, contact information

Problem

The pain that you're alleviating

Solution

An explanation of how you alleviate the pain; your value proposition

Business model

How you make money

Underlying magic

The technology and secret sauce behind your solution

Marketing and sales

How you are going to reach your customers

Competition

A complete view of the competitive landscape

Management team

The key players

Financials and metrics

Your projections

Current status

Where you are now, and how you will use the money you raise (as shown in Figure 8-4)

FIGURE 8-4

In an investor pitch deck, be sure to include your current status.

Make sure you answer the question, "What does this organization do?" *The Art of the Start* contains useful exercises and guides that any founder will find beneficial, including specific tips for using PowerPoint to design your pitch slidedeck.

Here are some additional tips from Garr Reynolds, author of *Presentation Zen: Simple Ideas on Presentation Design and Delivery* (New Riders), to help you create a winning demo day presentation:

- Study books on graphic design and visual communication to improve your visual literacy. Go for simple, captivating images.
- Choose 2-D graphs rather than 3-D graphs, because 3-D graphs are harder to read; the shadow creates distortion.
- When creating your presentation, think of the audience first. What do they need? What do you want to say that they need to hear? Focus on that as your core message.

By following these suggestions, you'll be well on your way to creating compelling, memorable presentations.

Startup Summary Tips

▶ Develop slidedecks specifically tailored to investors and demo days to put yourself in the best position to get engagement and secure funding.

▶ Focus your slides on what the audience needs and what they need to hear from you.

▶ Begin with the problem statement and keep the tone of your presentation in mind; get the audience to buy into the problem.

▶ Explain clearly what your startup can do.

▶ End memorably.

SlideShare for Nonprofits

Nonprofits can experience the same benefits as for-profit companies in the areas of content marketing discussed in Chapter 5, and the resources described in Chapter 6 about research and collaboration also apply in many cases. Conducting research on SlideShare can make purchasing decisions easier. The knowledge, tutorials, and analysis shared by millions of SlideShare users are a valuable free resource for nonprofits that lack the funds to hire a consultant to help them find what they need.

Nonprofits face many of the same challenges as for-profit businesses, such as raising funding and differentiating from similar groups (or, as the B Corporation calls them, *pretenders*). There's the need to continuously grow awareness and attract supporters and users of the organizations' services, all while staying true to the organization's mission and vision—also known as *branding* and *public perception*.

In 2012, NTEN, Common Ground, and Blackbaud conducted their fourth annual Nonprofit Social Networking Benchmark Report. This extensive survey provides valuable information about the behavior and trends surrounding social networking within nonprofits and businesses that serve the nonprofit sector. One important finding of the study ranked the success factors of organizations using social media, as shown in Figure 8-5.

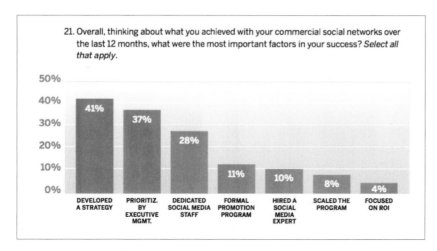

21. Overall, thinking about what you achieved with your commercial social networks over the last 12 months, what were the most important factors in your success? *Select all that apply.*

FIGURE 8-5
The Nonprofit
Social Networking
Benchmark
Report ranked the
success factors of
nonprofits using
social media.

DEVELOPING STRATEGY

Nonprofits can use SlideShare to take advantage of the two top factors in creating a successful social network: developing a strategy and getting executive commitment. Here's how:

- Create an editorial calendar with a schedule for developing slidedecks and embedding those slidedecks in blog posts. Include presentations in your overall content and social media strategy.
- Create a series of slidedecks based on a theme, establishing your organization as a subject matter expert and as a current, relevant resource in your community.
- Get executive buy-in for the value of slidedecks by uploading slidedecks from recent presentations given by directors and board members. Use SlideShare analytics and LeadShare to monitor views and downloads and generate inquiries about your programs.
- Create and upload regular slideshows with a recurring theme, such as the National Trust for Historic Preservation has done with its "Ten on Tuesday" series.

[TIP]   Create a Regular-Interval Slideshow

Every Tuesday, the National Trust for Historic Preservation (NTHP) uploads a slideshow (see Figure 8-6) that builds a collection of content, adds value to its stakeholders, and keeps the NTHP name and content in front of existing and potential members and benefactors. The presentations contain roughly 12 slides, a reasonable amount of content to create on a regular basis. The theme and design are consistent, which strengthens the brand design and message.

FIGURE 8-6
A regular series of presentations quickly generates a collection of content.

By following this advice, nonprofits develop a sound editorial strategy for getting their content out on a timely, regular basis. Adhering to a regular publication schedule, along with showcasing presentations by board members and tracking their views and activities, builds executive enthusiasm and support.

CREATING COMMUNITY

It's no surprise that nonprofits have embraced social media and interactive media to accomplish their goals. Slideshows help connect organizations to those with similar missions, creating a community of nonprofit practitioners.

Publishing and promoting content across multiple channels is important for reaching as many people in your community as possible. In their book *101 Social Media Tactics for Nonprofits* (Wiley), Melanie Mathos and Chad Norman write:

Social media engagement is one of the best ways to get supporters hooked on your mission or further entrench them if they're already fans. Every action they take on your behalf or interaction they have with your staff pushes them closer and closer to becoming a lifelong supporter who donates, joins, or volunteers.

The nonprofit Swiss institution New Cities Foundation found this to be true when it received runner-up in *BtoB Magazine*'s People's Choice social awards for its DeusM social media campaign.

With a small staff working across multiple channels, the one-month campaign drove a 20% increase in conference registrations. Facebook likes tripled, Twitter mentions rose nearly fivefold, and content on SlideShare and Scribd was viewed more than 20,000 times. Targeted Facebook advertising and conventional press releases supported the effort; 247 outlets picked up the formal conference release. New Cities Foundation also publishes presentations from guest speakers at its member events.

Amy Sample Ward is an author, facilitator, and trainer focused on leveraging social technologies for social change. Here's what Amy has to say about using SlideShare:

SlideShare reminds me of YouTube in that many nonprofits and even individuals use YouTube as the online storage space for videos that they plan to embed on their website or blog and otherwise share across the Web. You benefit by storing the videos in a public and popular place so those that aren't already watching your website can still come across your video and get engaged. SlideShare, with that many views, is serving a similar purpose where users are uploading content to be stored on SlideShare that they intend to embed or share elsewhere but benefit from those on the platform coming across the material and learning more.

Another highlight is the organic search traffic that nonprofits should take more advantage of. Have you spent days putting together a presentation for your board or a potential funder that highlights your work and impact? Maybe it outlines how a new program is going to make a specific change to your community or the world. Putting that presentation on SlideShare where the title and the slide material can be indexed for searches means the next time I'm online searching for "important programs to end homelessness in NYC" I find your slides, your ideas, and ways to get involved with your organization.

It's also noteworthy the high percentage of business and organizational leaders using SlideShare. Even more reason to expect that those coming across your material there to be potential partners, donors, or volunteers.

In short, SlideShare helps nonprofits reach new potential donors who might not otherwise know about the organization. Nonprofits also use SlideShare to report out to existing donors. Finally, nonprofits use SlideShare to share best practices across locations, such as how to make the best use of their volunteers.

DEVELOPING THE ORGANIZATION

Beth Kanter has been a SlideShare power user since 2006. As coauthor of *The Networked Nonprofit* and *Measuring the Networked Nonprofit* (both Jossey-Bass), Beth is an active and sought-after public speaker. In *Measuring the Networked Nonprofit*, Beth defines four steps in the maturation of a nonprofit using social media, shown in Figure 8-7.

FIGURE 8-7
Nonprofits go through four stages in their evolution toward social networking maturity.

Becoming A Networked Nonprofit: Maturity of Practice Model: Overview

Crawl	Walk	Run	Fly
Time Investment	Link Social to Communications Objective	Integrated Content Strategy	Integrated Multiple Channels
Culture change	Social Media Policy	Engage Influencers and Partners	Network Building
Basics	Small Pilots for Insights and Practice	Best Practices in Tactics Tangible Results	Reflection, Continually Improve Results

Presentations can be used in each stage of this evolution:

Crawl

Create a slideshow introducing your organization, team, and key principles.

Walk

Create slideshows that describe how your organization uses social media, upgrade to a PRO account, and experiment with LeadShare to generate inquiries.

Run

Include presentations in your content strategy and editorial calendar. Create a template to streamline the design process and visually brand the organization.

Fly

Publish slideshows on your Facebook and LinkedIn pages, embed slidedecks in your blog posts, and encourage bloggers for other organizations to embed your presentations. Monitor SlideShare analytics to see what generates the most views, shares, and downloads.

Take advantage of the half-price discount that SlideShare offers nonprofits. This will give you access to the analytics tools that allow you to measure your presentations' activity. Beth has identified four desired results, shown in Figure 8-8, that nonprofits should measure in order to understand their content's value.

Measuring Your Content: To What End?		
Result	**Metrics**	**Analysis Question**
Consumption	Views Reach Followers	Does your audience care about the topics your content covers? Are they consuming your content?
Engagement	Retweets Shares Comments	Does your content mean enough to your audience for them to share it or engage with it?
Action	Referrals Sign Ups Phone Calls	Does your content help you achieve your goals?
Revenue	Dollars Donors Volunteers	Does your content help you raise money, recruit volunteers or save time?

FIGURE 8-8
Nonprofits should measure these four results.

Here is how Beth sees the value of her SlideShare channel:

Presentations and instructional content are an important part of my content strategy and the lifeblood of my work as a trainer. SlideShare helps set my work free and share it with nonprofit professionals all over the world.

My content on SlideShare can easily be published on my blog or by anyone else anyplace else! I also share my SlideShare content in my other social streams. For example, I share them on my welcome tab on my Facebook page and on my LinkedIn profile. As a speaker and trainer, SlideShare—along with wikis, Twitter, and other tools—is an important part of my trainer's social media toolbox.

Nonprofits can follow Beth's advice and use SlideShare in a phased approach, adding steps and activities as they build experience with the medium. See the "Real-World Example" with Beth Kanter for nine ways that nonprofits can use SlideShare.

[REAL-WORLD EXAMPLE] Beth Kanter

 In her now-classic blog post, "*Nine Ways Networked Nonprofits Use SlideShare*" (*http://bit.ly/bz7NyD*), Beth encourages nonprofits to take advantage of SlideShare in the following ways:

1. Networked Professional Development and Learning

Three years ago, I wrote a post about how SlideShare supports networked learning and networked professional development. This is what Nancy White is calling "Triangulating Professional Learning." It's the ability to learn from professionals inside and outside of your field. As SlideShare has excellent social media content, I can view slideshows across different types of industries and networks. I don't have [to] be a networked silo!

2. Discover, Interact, and Learn from Thought Leaders

I love the fact that I can see slide presentations from some [of] my favorite thinkers in the social media field, literally hours before or after they've given the presentation. For example, David Armano, Dave McClure, and Guy Kawasaki. But you can also find rock star thought leaders in your field publishing their decks to SlideShare. For example, Amy Sample Ward, Danielle Brigida, and Michael Edson. And it isn't just individuals. You can grab the most recent research from the Pew Internet and American Life Center.

3. Informal Collaboration with Peers

One of the best experiences I ever had learning and collaborating with peers was setting up a sand box for network weavers.

4. Create an Archive for Conference Presentations

Perhaps the most common use of SlideShare by nonprofits is setting up groups or events to collect conference presentations in one place so participants can find them. I like the fact that I can find the presentations from sessions I attended as well as those from sessions I didn't attend. Some events have set up branded channels, like the Bar Camp Channel.

5. Share Draft Documents and Get Feedback

The Red Cross used SlideShare to share its social media policy and get feedback.

6. Training

Nonprofits that offer training as one of their programs have embraced SlideShare. These include CanadaHelps, Npower Michigan, and Michigan Nonprofit Association. NTEN's WeAreMedia project has taken this a step further and uses SlideShare so trainers can remix each other's decks.

7. Fundraising

I have not come across too many organizations using SlideShare for fundraising, although I've seen a few breathtaking decks created by "free agent" fundraisers for disaster relief efforts over the years. These include: Nargis Cyclone and China Earthquake.

8. Advocacy

These have come in the form of awareness events like Earth Hour and Yoga to End Poverty.

9. Sharing Your Organization's Story

National Wildlife Federation uses SlideShare for its presentations, but also to promote the winners of their photo contests. The Counterpart uses SlideShare to share its annual report information. Monitor Institute shared a PDF of its case study on how Kaboom! is scaling its social impact. ◆

RECRUITING VOLUNTEERS

Nonprofits often face the challenging task of recruiting volunteers. Publishing on SlideShare benefits from the site's high Google ranking as a trusted destination, reaching potential new volunteers (or donors) who don't know about the organization. What's more, nonprofits can use SlideShare's visual medium to tell a more compelling story. For example, Chelsea Martin, Program Manager at Volunteer Centers of Michigan, uses a photo of a little girl with the targeted question: "Would you be my mentor?" The photo captures attention and the text is a specific call to action.

You can also use SlideShare to describe volunteer positions. The key is to be specific so that volunteers can find you and *self-screen* based on their personal interests and skills. For example, write the title of the position, its objective location, and the responsibilities you're looking for. Include the time commitment required and whether you'll provide any training or support. Later, you can also use SlideShare to upload your training programs!

Another way to entice volunteers is to tell the success stories of your existing volunteers. This is a double-win, because honoring your volunteers in a public forum like SlideShare builds their loyalty while at the same time explaining to others the roles volunteers play. Highlight volunteers' significant moments and recognize those who went above and beyond what was needed.

Finally, time your uploads with national days of service, such as National Volunteer Week or Martin Luther King Day to capture news media attention as well.

Nonprofit Summary Tips

▶ Post photo slideshows of fundraising events and community activities.

▶ Highlight members. Designate a "volunteer of the month" and create a short slideshow describing the person, her activities, and some photos of her in action. At the end of the year, create a year-end slideshow of the monthly volunteers of the month.

▶ Show the positive impact of the organization. Create a slideshow that includes photos and maps of the area affected by your efforts. Include some slides with photos and testimonials of beneficiaries, and some easy-to-digest graphs showing progress.

▶ Promote an event or activity: announce your next event, include the benefits of participating and photos of preparations, and don't forget to link to registration details.

▶ Publish slideshows from partners, especially when presented at your events, to show your presence in the community and leverage your partners' social networks.

SlideShare for Journalists

Journalists, like so many other professionals affected by the growth of digital media, are challenged to find new ways to remain relevant and current. The introduction of citizen journalists has broadened the number of ordinary people who are able to create content and capture visual images accompanying it. The increasing number of citizen journalists has flattened the process in which news media is published.

Trained, professional journalists often use the same online publishing platforms as their amateur counterparts, though the quality and accuracy of the content getting published from citizen journalists lacks the editorial step that previously ensured (or at least enhanced) its quality. As a trade-off, however, a breaking-news story has the advantage of immediacy when the general population uploads directly to YouTube, tweets details as it happens, and curates a summary of the event using sites like SlideShare.

Instead of having the umbrella of traditional news networks, many journalists are now freelance writers, photographers, and videographers. They are valued by the size of their audience, in addition to the quality of their stories and access to sources.

Instead of *pushing* news out to the masses, journalists must now *engage* with the general public. Journalists who get on board with social media are the most likely to find success, not only for getting story ideas and information, but also for having their news stories shared and distributed by their social media followers.

Disruption has occurred not because of the technology, but also because of the general public's use of the technology. Citizens are empowered and motivated to capture the news happening in their lives and communities.

Instead of a news story leading to content creation, now content creates the news story. In the past, professional media created news, which led to content and commentary by others. Now, a distributed crowd creates content that can go viral and become news. The traditional flow of information is inverted, from news created by a few and read by many to news created by many that's picked up by the news sources.

THE EVOLUTION OF NEW MEDIA

Jim Long (@*newmediajim* on Twitter) has grown his online identity from behind the camera to in front of the audience. As lead cameraman and content creator for NBC News, Jim has traveled the world with US presidents, from war zones to historic diplomatic meetings. Here's how Jim describes the evolution of news media in the past decade:

> *I see the social web transform our assumptions about media—who controls it, who creates it, and who profits from it. I watch as blogging, podcasting, Twitter—these tools of social currency—shift millions of peoples' attention from the media brands they grew up with to content created by neighbors, friends, or strangers across the globe. Now, people participate with, respond to, and challenge their media.*

> *While lowered production costs have allowed many to enter the media production field, it is the Internet that has made distribution and syndication simple, allowing anyone to easily connect audiences with custom-tailored content. This trend that began only a few years ago continues to shift the power structure in media today.*

Jim has chosen to diversify his professional attention and has created his own media company in anticipation of the overlap between web video and traditional broadcast TV.

The ability to embed video within a presentation and then publish it on SlideShare provides a rich opportunity for journalists, as well as broadcast networks, to broaden their reach. The same benefits of SEO and exponential sharing apply to news as much as they do to content marketing or other types of media distribution.

As journalists become increasingly independent, their news stories and the platforms on which they publish news become part of their professional profiles. Journalists can demonstrate their reporting and publishing capabilities by creating presentations, publishing them on SlideShare, and pulling them into their LinkedIn profiles, as marketing executive Tery Spataro has done in Figure 8-9.

A number of institutions within the journalism community understand the rapid changes taking place in the field. Several have made a commitment to bringing both their existing members and emerging journalists up to speed on digital and social media trends and best practices.

Summary

I'm a marketer that provides digital & tech experiences to bring brands to life while delighting and engaging customers.

Passionate about using digital & technology to create ideas that innovate, communicate, promote brands or change the physical environment. I provide digital/technology marketing strategies for brands with a focus on promotion, innovation, communication or in-store retail. I held executive positions with well-known agencies, or I am brought on by an agency or business as an expert consultant in digital/technology marketing.

Clients enjoy my style of leadership, in which I enjoy inspiring and educating them on emerging trends in digital and technology. I mentor my employees by grooming them to be successful in their positions, helping them see long term bigger picture.

Tery Spataro Bio-Graph | Digital Strategy by Tery Spataro

For example, National Public Radio (NPR) Digital Network has published presentations on SlideShare with topics ranging from Webcast Metrics to how its popular program *Fresh Air* uses social media. NPR Digital's *"9 Types of Local Stories that Cause Engagement"* (*http://bit.ly/VbSS3E*) summarizes a three-month survey of which types of stories received the most shares, likes, and comments. NPR Digital's findings, shown in Figure 8-10, are relevant for journalists and any content creator who wants to increase audience engagement.

Furthermore, three journalism centers offer training for journalists via their SlideShare channels:

FIGURE 8-9
Show examples of your work and expertise with presentations on your LinkedIn profile.

Journalism Interactive

A partnership between the University of Maryland and the University of Florida, Journalism Interactive publishes slidedecks from its annual conference to its SlideShare channel. Useful information about getting a job, personal branding, functional artwork, and four-dimensional storytelling can all be found in the presentations from this event.

Reynolds Center for Business Journalism

The Reynolds Center for Business Journalism shares more than 230 presentations on its SlideShare channel. Topics include how to find a business story, how to mine economic data, and how to use multimedia in reporting.

Knight Digital Media Center (KDMC) at UC Berkeley

The KDMC conducts hands-on training for journalists in the form of weeklong workshops. It shares presentations of a more technical nature on its SlideShare channel.

In short, SlideShare is a source of education on the evolution of new media and digital journalism, as well as a means by which journalists can showcase their talents and reach a wider audience.

FIGURE 8-10
NPR Digital shares
its user research.

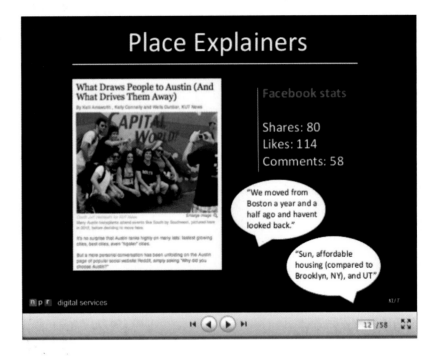

GETTING THE WORD OUT

Alex Balfour was the head of new media for the London 2012 Olympics. Given the large role that social and digital media played during the event, the analytics from this activity was of great interest to many business, sports, and marketing professionals.

Instead of releasing a traditional report made up of text and numbers, Alex aggregated the data and included it with photos to tell the whole story of the Olympic Games and online activity surrounding the Games. The data guides a timeline that ties the events and activities together. It also presents specific data, such as the most popular athlete profile pages, shown in Figure 8-11.

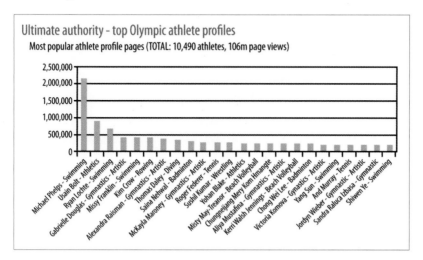

FIGURE 8-11
Alex Balfour's presentation shares analytics from the London 2012 Olympics.

The slideshow shares the benchmark statistics on use of electronic devices, ambition, and goals for interaction, as well as how well the digital media team's efforts measured up. The information and the story in this slideshow appealed to many journalists and blogs, as demonstrated by its 66,000+ views and nearly 170 embeds, all from one slideshow.

HIGHLIGHTING MARGINALIZED POPULATIONS

For minorities and marginalized populations, publishing slideshows to SlideShare is a powerful way to reach out to the mainstream, first-world population. It is also an effective method for getting the attention of journalists.

The Kenyan-based International Livestock Research Institute (ILRI), for example, works at the crossroads of livestock and poverty, bringing high-quality science and capacity building to bear on poverty reduction and sustainable development. The ILRI has uploaded nearly 1,000 slideshows to its SlideShare account, a testimony to SlideShare's importance in ILRI's communication strategy.

For journalists who are looking for research, anecdotes, and photographs of poverty anywhere in the world and the role of livestock, the ILRI SlideShare channel provides everything that is available to share, such as research results informing the Women's Empowerment Agriculture Index (WEAI), shown in Figure 8-12.

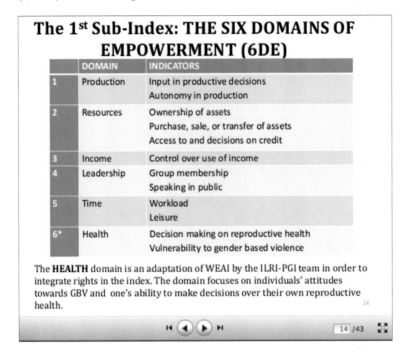

The 1st Sub-Index: THE SIX DOMAINS OF EMPOWERMENT (6DE)

	DOMAIN	INDICATORS
1	Production	Input in productive decisions Autonomy in production
2	Resources	Ownership of assets Purchase, sale, or transfer of assets Access to and decisions on credit
3	Income	Control over use of income
4	Leadership	Group membership Speaking in public
5	Time	Workload Leisure
6*	Health	Decision making on reproductive health Vulnerability to gender based violence

The **HEALTH** domain is an adaptation of WEAI by the ILRI-PGI team in order to integrate rights in the index. The domain focuses on individuals' attitudes towards GBV and one's ability to make decisions over their own reproductive health.

14 / 43

CROWDSOURCING AND SOCIAL JOURNALISM

Mandy Jenkins of Digital First Media embraces the public nature of today's online news. She shares insights and recommendations for journalists in the areas of personal branding, social media, and strategy. She encourages journalists to use *crowdsourcing* (soliciting and compiling small contributions from many individual sources) to get relevant information for their news stories and gives tips for efficiently using social media to crowdsource, as shown in Figure 8-13.

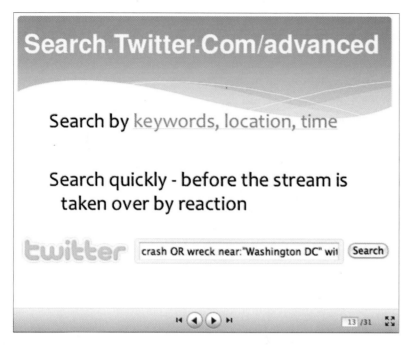

FIGURE 8-13
Mandy Jenkins
shares tutorial
presentations to
help journalists
learn how to
crowdsource.

When putting together a blog post news story, create a presentation that summarizes the story and include photos and a map of where your crowdsourced information originated, as Mandy does in Figure 8-14.

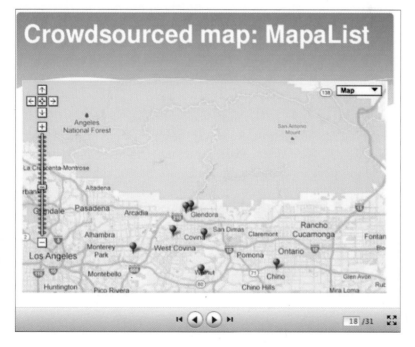

FIGURE 8-14
Maps are a great
way to show the
location of your
sources.

Here are Mandy Jenkins's *eight rules of social journalism* (*http://slidesha. re/XzZ571*):

- Respond to replies, comments, and questions (especially questions) everywhere.
- Be transparent in all you do.
- Ask for help when you need it.
- Be thankful.
- Make corrections quickly and publicly.
- Address criticism without spats.
- Be consistent.
- Don't just push your content out; share other links, too.

CURATORS AS THE NEW EDITORS

The perception of news stories is strongly affected by the images and text that are selected to tell them. The Web is continuously updated with images, videos, and text that describe current events, often as they occur. The originator of these pieces of information often uploads them before fully understanding what he is reporting. As the pieces of content come together, the story unfolds. Gathering these pieces and putting them together to form a presentation is like putting together the pieces of a puzzle. This is where *curation* becomes the editor of new journalism.

Immediately after the 2012 presidential election, marketing executive Rohit Bhargava reached out to his social networks and asked people to submit links to their favorite campaign photographs. He was assessing the importance of "likeability" in the election outcome. Rohit collected and assembled the photos in a slideshow, visually comparing the nature of the two campaigns, as shown Figure 8-15.

By pairing photographs of President Obama with those of Governor Romney in similar contexts, Rohit saw the photographs begin to tell a story. Rohit created a few slides to give context for his findings, and then he let the remaining 36 slides of photographs support those findings.

FIGURE 8-15
Crowdsourced photos illustrate the differences in candidates during the 2012 election.

PUBLISHING NEWS ON SLIDESHARE

Steve Buttry is one of the most influential leaders embracing the disruption of traditional journalism and the use of new media. On his blog, Buttry Diary, Steve shared these tips for journalists using SlideShare (*http://bit. ly/12N32uC*):

- *Content is more important than appearance.*
- *Social tools help you achieve more than your purpose. I post slides primarily as a follow-up reference for the people attending my workshop. But SlideShare, helped by Twitter and other people embedding the slides on blogs, extends the learning to many more people.*

- *Keep your slides simple, your words few, and your fonts large. Except for the too-long leads in my workshop on writing leads (http://www.slideshare.net/stevebuttry/make-every-word-count), I try to present a few simple points that echo or supplement what I'm saying.*
- *Don't read your slides to the group you're presenting to. They can read. Look at them and talk. (I try to position myself so I can see the slides on my laptop and they function as my notes, but I don't read them and I don't look at the screen.)*
- *Tell workshop participants that you're posting the slides to SlideShare (or on your blog), so you don't need to worry about advancing a slide before they've been able to copy down all your points.*
- *If you have a blog post related to the slides, be sure to add the link to the text accompanying your slides. I often forget this. Since I embed the slides in the blog post, I upload the slides first, before I have the link. Then I forget to go back and add the link.*

Steve's frank and honest (at times almost confessional) style provides pointers for journalists while helping them avoid easy-to-make mistakes.

In summary, journalists can use SlideShare as a research tool, as a publishing platform, and as a way to extend their online portfolio and media presence. When creating your SlideShare presence, be consistent in your branding—that is, use your name as it typically appears in your bylines, use photos that you use in other online professional settings (such as LinkedIn), and use the colors, fonts, and design style you use in your other branding efforts, such as your website. The consistency will make your content more recognizable across the platforms on which you publish, strengthening your reputation and extending your reach.

Journalist Summary Tips

▶ Use SlideShare to track the evolution of digital journalism and new media.

▶ Build your personal platform on SlideShare to develop your own brand and name recognition.

▶ Journalists in developing countries can use SlideShare to reach the developed world more effectively.

▶ Journalists covering emerging nations can use SlideShare to get research and first-hand information that may be difficult to find elsewhere.

▶ The first-person, citizen-publication aspect of SlideShare means that journalists can often find real-time, eyewitness stories such as of major disasters like Hurricane Sandy.

SlideShare for Government

The size of the SlideShare audience provides a perfect opportunity for government agencies supporting open government and transparency. Agencies in the public sector can upload presentations in a timely manner, sharing them easily with an audience much larger than they would reach by publishing only on the department's website.

Government agencies are often tasked with making public documents available to constituents and collecting public feedback. Publishing these materials on SlideShare allows them to reach a much broader set of constituents. It also allows viewers to offer comments right on the presentation page. Agency staff easily can track the number of times the presentations or documents are viewed.

ONE-STOP PUBLIC SECTOR PUBLISHING

Here are some of the types of documents and presentations that government agencies are publishing on SlideShare:

- Budgets and other documents for public review
- Emergency plans and contact information
- Proposed changes in public areas, such as roadways and parks
- Press releases
- Brochures and promotional materials
- Photo slideshows of public service events

Just as in the private sector, measuring the access and interaction with documents and presentations is an important way of gauging public sentiment. SlideShare analytics enable agencies to track the effectiveness and popularity of published materials by measuring the number of:

- Views of content
- Views of embedded presentations
- Locations online where the content is embedded
- Shares on social media platforms
- Downloads of the material
- Favorites

Government agencies can satisfy these outreach requirements for public review and input by publishing documents and presentations on SlideShare, which has the added benefits of:

- Increasing efficiency and expedite document distribution.
- Reducing staff time spent distributing documents via email.
- Saving time during the approval process by sharing documents and presentations internally with password protection before releasing to the public.

Public agencies at every level of government have official channels on SlideShare. The following sections show examples of how government organizations are publishing presentations to achieve their goals of outreach and transparency across all levels of government, from local to state and regional to federal.

LOCAL GOVERNMENT

Fairfax County, Virginia, uses presentations as a tool for reaching citizens in the county. Fairfax County publishes presentations about a wide range of issues—everything from work safety to road widening to animal shelter updates.

The County also creates and shares presentations about issues in the community, such as homelessness and public health. It uploads presentations with project status reports. It also provides an economic and demographic overview presentation in its strategy to attract new businesses to Fairfax County.

STATE GOVERNMENT

The State of Utah shares presentations that address economic developments and public safety, health, and quality of life. The State is creating an archive of public documents by publishing annual reports, such as the Utah Geological Survey Notes.

Utah includes SlideShare in its communication channels for publishing items like the Utah Child Protection Registry. By publishing materials like its magazine *TrendLines*, it strengthens the brand of the State of Utah. SlideShare as a publishing platform for presentations and documents is part of Utah's award-winning digital strategy for communications and public outreach.

Similarly, the Virginia Department of Business Assistance (VDBA) supports business formation and expansion in the Commonwealth of Virginia, as shown in Figure 8-16.

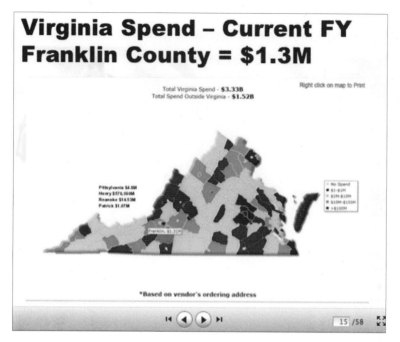

FIGURE 8-16
Virginia publishes
presentations as
part of its outreach
strategy.

As the business services manager in the agency's Abingdon office serving 23 localities in southwest Virginia, Sandy Ratliff publishes presentations and workshop materials that help new and expanding businesses. Not only are these materials shared with the public, but the department also promotes future events by offering a preview of what a workshop attendee can expect to learn.

REGIONAL AND MULTIJURISDICTIONAL GOVERNMENT

The Navajo Nation extends into the states of Utah, Arizona, and New Mexico, covering over 27,000 square miles. With such a broad geographic area of responsibility, the Navajo Nation uses SlideShare to make documents and communications available to its widely distributed citizens. Its Washington, DC, office publishes presentations about all kinds of topics, such as federal lending opportunities, claim settlements, and water rights, as shown in Figure 8-17.

As a city-county government agency, the Nashville Metropolitan Planning Organization shares presentations that address the region's long-range transportation plan and short-range transportation improvement program in order to engage citizens as stakeholders.

FIGURE 8-17

Multijurisdictional
agencies need
to reach citizens
in dispersed
geographic areas.

FIGURE 8-17
Multijurisdictional agencies need to reach citizens in dispersed geographic areas.

FEDERAL GOVERNMENT TRANSPARENCY

In 2009, the White House issued the *Open Government Directive (http://1.usa.gov/4sbQJk)*, which was sent to the head of every federal department and agency. It instructed the agencies to take specific actions to open their operations to the public. The directive states:

> *Agencies shall respect the presumption of openness by publishing information online (in addition to any other planned or mandated publication methods) and by preserving and maintaining electronic information, consistent with the Federal Records Act and other applicable law and policy. Timely publication of information is an essential component of transparency.*

The White House has established its SlideShare network as a platform for open government with the timely sharing of documents and presentations. As the White House continues to reach a more digital constituency, it publishes interactive slideshows like the ones used during President Obama's State of the Union addresses in 2012 and 2013, as shown in Figure 8-18.

FIGURE 8-18
The White House supplements the State of the Union address with a presentation on SlideShare.

The Congressional Budget Office (CBO) provides timely analyses of issues affecting the federal budget. As a catalyst for open government and transparency, the CBO's official channel on SlideShare, shown in Figure 8-19, allows it to publish information publicly, ensuring that members of Congress and US citizens have access.

The US Department of Energy demonstrates transparency by publishing its budget and plans with presentations on SlideShare. In addition, it provides information that is of interest to the American people, but not necessarily within the US jurisdiction, such as radiation reports from the Fukushima nuclear power plant after the 2011 earthquake and tsunami in Japan.

The National Prevention Information Network (NPIN) serves prevention partners of the Center for Disease Control. NPIN is a clearinghouse that collects and disseminates data and materials to support the work of prevention organizations and workers in international, national, state, and local settings. The network facilitates program collaboration in sharing information, resources, published materials, research, and trends. It also promotes the use of social media and provides educational presentations about using social media in public health, as shown in Figure 8-20.

FIGURE 8-19
The Congressional Budget Office uses SlideShare as a communications channel.

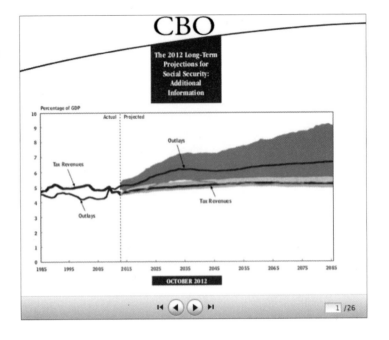

FIGURE 8-20
NPIN trains its members on social media with presentations on SlideShare.

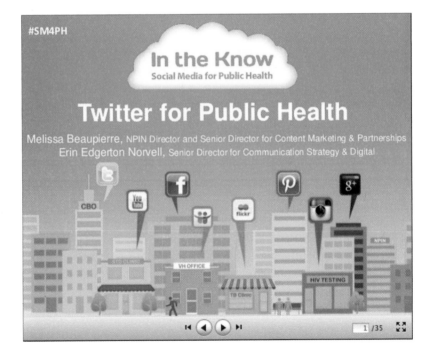

PUBLIC/PRIVATE PRESENTATIONS

Some organizations and private-sector companies are suppliers and partners of public-sector agencies. For example, as the nation's central bank, the Federal Reserve System formulates monetary policy, serves as a bank regulator, administers certain consumer protection laws, and is the fiscal agent for the US government. Its Economic Education Group publishes presentations that are used by teachers to educate students about money and economics, such as the Money Supply presentation shown in Figure 8-21.

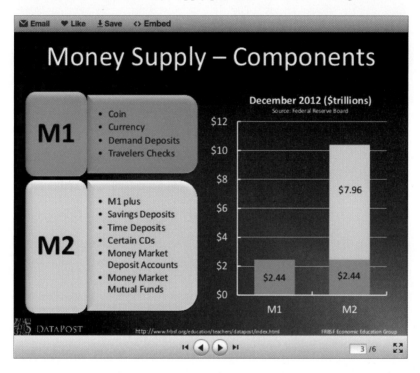

FIGURE 8-21
The Federal Reserve offers educational tools in the form of presentations.

DigitalGlobe is a global provider of commercial high-resolution earth imagery products and services. Through images from its own satellites, DigitalGlobe supports a wide variety of uses within defense and intelligence, civil agencies, mapping and analysis, environmental monitoring, oil and gas exploration, infrastructure management, Internet portals, and navigation technology.

Accordingly, DigitalGlobe is often called upon to present at government conferences, such as the White House Open Data for Development Conference (known as the Global Development Data Jam), where DigitalGlobe experts partnered with White House CTO Todd Park to present an overview of the Water Wells for Africa program, shown in Figure 8-22.

FIGURE 8-22
DigitalGlobe and the White House collaborated on a presentation about Open Data.

GovLoop is the "Knowledge Network for Government," an online community connecting over 60,000 public-sector professionals. GovLoop works with top *industry partners (http://www.govloop.com/page/partner-resources)*—including Google, HP, Microsoft, and IBM—to provide resources and tools (such as guides, infographics, online training, and educational events) for public-sector professionals. GovLoop is active on SlideShare, providing resources for connecting with professional peers, sharing best practices, and finding career-building opportunities.

Governmental organizations from all over the world upload presentations, documents, and videos on SlideShare. To see more ways that public agencies are publishing content, click the Browse button on the SlideShare home page, scroll down to Channels, and select Government/Military.

Government Summary Tips

▶ Use SlideShare to quickly and easily distribute documents for public review.

▶ Make presentations, forms, and documents available 24/7.

▶ Reach constituents on the platform they are most likely to use by sharing to the agency's other social sites.

▶ Supplement print and broadcast distribution of materials online via SlideShare.

▶ Provide transparency with presentations and documents published on SlideShare, which can be downloaded and embedded on the websites and blogs of private citizens and the media.

▶ Facilitate public commentary. Public agencies can satisfy the review and public comment requirements by publishing and gathering comments on SlideShare.

▶ Easily track comments because comments are published on the presentation or document's SlideShare page, keeping them in one place and making them available for public review.

▶ Publish presentations and meeting notes to reach stakeholders who could not attend the meeting.

▶ Embed the presentations on the public agency's website.

Index

About the Authors

As the community manager and editor for SlideShare from 2010 to 2013, **Kit Seeborg** curated and featured presentations on the SlideShare home page, wrote and edited its blog and newsletters, and represented Slide-Share on Facebook, Twitter, LinkedIn, and Google+. SlideShare CEO Rashmi Sinha refers to Kit as the "voice of SlideShare." She continues to engage with the world's leading experts in presentation trends, design, and delivery. Kit is also founder of the digital music licensing company, BumperTunes. She has worked extensively in digital media and communications, producing live video webcasts for Fortune 100 companies, planning industry events, and speaking at conferences such as WebVisions and South by Southwest.

Andrea Meyer is an award-winning speaker, writer, and ghostwriter. Known for her practical, "how-to" presentation style, she has traveled to 40 countries speaking and writing about innovation and how to get breakthrough insights. She founded Working Knowledge.com in 1988, and her clients include IBM, Cisco, MIT, Harvard, McKinsey & Co., InnoCentive, AARP, and OECD. Andrea has contributed to 35 books on business, innovation, and psychology. She is a member, officer and area governor of Toastmasters International. She's very active in social media and is a Certified Online Instructor and a high-profile innovation blogger. Andrea has an M.S. in Information Science, is a member of Mensa, and is listed in Who's Who in America.

Photos by Nathan Lotz

Have it your way.

O'Reilly eBooks

- Lifetime access to the book when you buy through oreilly.com
- Provided in up to four DRM-free file formats, for use on the devices of your choice: PDF, .epub, Kindle-compatible .mobi, and Android .apk
- Fully searchable, with copy-and-paste and print functionality
- Alerts when files are updated with corrections and additions

oreilly.com/ebooks/

Safari Books Online

- Access the contents and quickly search over 7000 books on technology, business, and certification guides
- Learn from expert video tutorials, and explore thousands of hours of video on technology and design topics
- Download whole books or chapters in PDF format, at no extra cost, to print or read on the go
- Get early access to books as they're being written
- Interact directly with authors of upcoming books
- Save up to 35% on O'Reilly print books

See the complete Safari Library at safari.oreilly.com

O'REILLY®

Spreading the knowledge of innovators.　　　　oreilly.com

Get even more for your money.

Join the O'Reilly Community, and register the O'Reilly books you own. It's free, and you'll get:

- $4.99 ebook upgrade offer
- 40% upgrade offer on O'Reilly print books
- Membership discounts on books and events
- Free lifetime updates to ebooks and videos
- Multiple ebook formats, DRM FREE
- Participation in the O'Reilly community
- Newsletters
- Account management
- 100% Satisfaction Guarantee

Signing up is easy:

1. **Go to: oreilly.com/go/register**
2. **Create an O'Reilly login.**
3. **Provide your address.**
4. **Register your books.**

Note: English-language books only

To order books online:
oreilly.com/store

For questions about products or an order:
orders@oreilly.com

To sign up to get topic-specific email announcements and/or news about upcoming books, conferences, special offers, and new technologies:
elists@oreilly.com

For technical questions about book content:
booktech@oreilly.com

To submit new book proposals to our editors:
proposals@oreilly.com

O'Reilly books are available in multiple DRM-free ebook formats. For more information:
oreilly.com/ebooks

Spreading the knowledge of innovators   **oreilly.com**